D1623002

BILL MYERS

CHRIST B.C.

BECOMING CLOSER FRIENDS WITH THE
HIDDEN CHRIST OF THE OLD TESTAMENT

Regal Books
A Division of Gospel Light

Published by Regal Books
A Division of GL Publications
Ventura, California 93006
Printed in U.S.A.

Library of Congress Cataloging-in-Publication Data.

Myers, Bill, 1940-
    Christ, B.C. : becoming closer friends with the hidden Christ
of the Old Testament / Bill Myers.
    p.   cm.
    Summary: Examines the specific reference to Jesus Christ found
in the Old Testament and includes devotional readings.
    ISBN 0-8307-1304-2
    1. Teenagers—Prayer-books and devotions—English. [1.
Prayer books and devotions. 2. Christian life.] I. Title.
BV4850.M94   1990
232'.12—dc20   90-35816
                                                            CIP
                                                            AC

2 3 4 5 6 7 8 9 10 / 94 93 92 91

Rights for publishing this book in other languages are contracted by
Gospel Literature International (GLINT) foundation. GLINT also provides
technical help for the adaptation, translation, and publishing of Bible
study resources and books in scores of languages worldwide. For further
information, contact GLINT, Post Office Box 488, Rosemead, California,
91770, U.S.A., or the publisher.

TABLE OF CONTENTS

PREFACE

JUST A REMINDER

This is a daily devotional not a theological treatise.

Now, it's true, at the first of each week we'll take a look at some aspect of Jesus Christ in the Old Testament. But that's only for the first day or so. For the rest of that week we'll examine how that aspect applies to us today, now, where we live, where we go to school, where we go to work, where we love and fight and fear on a daily basis.

This is not a history lesson. It's a journey—an exploration. I pray that as you read each section over the next several weeks, this book will become an exploration into the infinite depths of Jesus Christ—an exploration that will make Him more personal in your day-to-day living—and, an exploration that will lead you deeper and deeper into the very center of His heart.

Bill Myers
Thousand Oaks, California

1
THE ROAD TO
UNDERSTANDING

Day 1
The Road to Emmaus

And beginning with Moses and all the Prophets,
he [Jesus] explained to them what was said in
all the Scriptures concerning himself.
Luke 24:27

Picture it. A man you believed to be God, a person you gave up everything to follow has just been destroyed. Evil has overcome good. Your whole purpose for living is gone. You are confused and feel betrayed by God. To sum it up, you just don't understand what's going on.

We've all been there, broken and confused by life, not understanding its whys or hows. And like the two disciples heading for Emmaus, we may even let our hopelessness cut us off from other believers and try to go it on our own. Thankfully, Jesus wasn't going to let them get away quite that easily. Not only did He track them down but He also shared with them what can only be described as the world's greatest Bible study. He literally went through the Old Testament and "explained...what was said in all the Scriptures concerning himself" (Luke 24:27).

There are different opinions about how many Old

Testament prophecies Jesus fulfilled when He was here on earth, but a safe guess is that it was well over 300. Three hundred Old Testament prophecies were directly fulfilled by Jesus! Everything from where He would be born, to where He'd live, to what He'd do, to when, where, how and why He would die.

Now it's true, some of these could just have been coincidences. But the chances of one man fulfilling *only 48* of the major prophecies would be: one out of 10,000, 000,000,000,000,000,000,000,000,000,000,000,000,000, 000,000,000,000,000,000,000,000,000,000,000,000,000, 000,000,000,000,000,000,000,000,000,000,000,000,000, 000,000,000,000,000,000,000,000,000![1] Jesus not only fulfilled those 48 but over 250 more. Plus He will be fulfilling hundreds more when He comes back the second time!

But Jesus' presence in the Old Testament is revealed by a lot more than hundreds of prophecies. In many ways His life, His ministry, His very personality saturate the books of the Old Testament. And why shouldn't they? If the Bible is the history of God's working with humankind, and since Jesus is God, then it only stands to reason we would see Him throughout.

Studying the Flood? What is it but an insight into Jesus' call for repentance, His wrath and His ultimate protection and mercy for those who have made Him Lord?

What is Exodus but an account of how Jesus works to set us free from the bondage of our flesh and our sins?

What is Joshua but an account of how Jesus helps us conquer the adversaries of our soul?

And the list goes on. With Jesus as the central character, passages that once seemed muddy and murky begin to take on new meaning. When we look for Christ we're no longer as lost, confused or (dare I say it) as bored.

It's as if we are on our own road to Emmaus surrounded by shadows and confusion about the Scriptures—until we begin to discover Jesus' presence in them. Then frequently those very Scriptures begin to take us into deeper understanding.

But Christ's work in helping us understand doesn't just end with Old Testament Scripture. As we'll see throughout the rest of this week, Jesus is the hub, the very foundation from which all true understanding begins.

Day 2
Understanding Scripture

The word of God is living and active. Sharper than any double-edged sword, it penetrates even to dividing soul and spirit, joints and marrow; it judges the thoughts and attitudes of the heart.
Hebrews 4:12

Next to God Himself there is no other being or force in the universe that has more power than His Word. In fact, according to Genesis, it was with His Word that He created the universe. (Not a bad display of power.) But that's just for starters!

According to 2 Timothy 3:16, all Scripture is "God-breathed." Somehow God's breath, His life, part of His very essence is supernaturally infused into the words of Scripture. With that in mind, the effect Scripture has on us mere mortals shouldn't be too surprising. In fact, with that in mind, it shouldn't surprise us that His Word can actually:

save us (see Jas. 1:21);
cleanse us (see Eph. 5:26);
encourage us (see Rom. 15:4);
give us faith (see Rom. 10:17);
equip us to do good (see 2 Tim. 3:17)
help us see ourselves as we really are (see Jas. 1:23-25).

When Jesus and Satan were battling it out in the desert (see Matt. 4) they probably could have used any weapon they wanted. But they decided to pass on the usual tools of warfare. Instead, the Creator of the universe and the most evil being in the universe used the most powerful weapon in the universe. They used one thing and one thing only: the Scriptures. Each time Satan tried to tempt Jesus by perverting God's Word, Jesus responded with the truth of that Word. In short, Christ defeated Satan by using "the sword of the Spirit, which is the word of God" (Eph. 6:17).

To me that says *power*—more power than I can even begin to imagine. But how can we plug into that power? How can you and I really absorb and understand the fullest and richest depths of that power?

The bad news is we can't—not on our own. You see Scripture is not a series of inert sentences that we can categorize, analyze and wrap up in a tidy little box (though many a theologian has tried). It is *living and active.* Once it gets into our souls, it moves about challenging and encouraging us in different ways at different times. Scripture is a living part of God (His breath) and to fully understand it would be as impossible as for us to fully understand God.

Yes, it's important to study Scripture, to use commentaries, to search for its literal meaning. But that's only the beginning. The real key to understanding Scripture is to put it into the hands of the Master Surgeon and ask Him to use it as He intended—to ask Him to use this tool that is *sharper than any double-edged sword* to cut away our dying flesh while nurturing and growing our eternal souls.

So, as important as the study of Scripture may be, it means nothing on its own. The only real understanding of Scripture comes as we ask the Lord to bring it to life personally.

There is much talk about the Holy Spirit's work in the Church today. But in the debates and discussions we frequently forget one of His primary jobs. Perhaps Jesus put it best in His farewell address to His disciples: "But when he, the Spirit of truth, comes, he will guide you into all truth" (John

16:13). He is our Tutor. He is our Instructor. He is our Guide.

All this to say: No matter how sincere and dedicated we may be in our pursuit to understand Scripture, our intellectual gymnastics will bring minimal results at best. Instead, the key is to go back to the road to Emmaus. We must once again depend upon the Lord. Like the disciples, we may be exhausted, perplexed, even angry at difficulties and confusion. But if we are willing to ask the Author for understanding, He is willing to breathe life into our understanding of His Words—which in turn breathes life into our souls.

Day 3
Understanding God

Here I am! I stand at the door and knock. If anyone hears my voice and opens the door, I will come in and eat with him, and he with me.
Revelation 3:20

If I had run out and asked the first woman I met to marry me she probably would have died laughing. Why? Because I'm such a strange and absurd character? Maybe. But more likely because she didn't know me.

How could we have solved that? We'd communicate. I'd talk, she'd listen. She'd talk, I'd listen. Gradually, we'd get to know each other. And, if the chemistry was right, we might fall in love.

That's what Christ wants. He wants us to know Him so deeply, understand Him so intimately, that we can't help but fall in love with Him.

Yet somehow we think we can short-circuit that understanding-and-falling-in-love process. We think that we can just sort of wake up one morning and instantly know Him, or at best show up once a week and listen to someone chatter about Him for 20 to 30 minutes and BINGO, instant love.

But knowing people through secondhand information is not really knowing them. Before I finally married, I got to know my wife-to-be personally. I did not rely on someone else's description. The same is true with God. There are no instant short cuts. The only way to really know Him and to really fall in love with Him is through personal, one-on-one *communication* with Him.

And, as obvious as it may sound, we communicate with God much the same way as we communicate with others. Through talking and listening.

Talking

The most common way of talking to God is through prayer. At the beginning stages we may treat prayer like a Christmas list and God as our private Santa Claus. Or as Bob Dylan sings, we may "think He's just an errand boy to satisfy [our] wandering desires."[2] But as we mature, we begin to understand deeper forms of prayer. We begin to experience the depths and mysteries that are unlocked through singing, worshiping and praising. Eventually we may even begin to experience the intense peace of just sitting quietly before Him in awe.

But expressing ourselves is only half of the communication process. The other half lies in...

Listening

The most obvious way of listening to God is through His Word. We've already discussed the power Scripture has to transform our lives. But the transformation doesn't stop there. People who are transformed by Scripture are often used by God to help in His transformation of others. I know people who have made tremendous changes in the world who simply point to the few minutes a day they spend with Scripture as a major source of their strength.

Then there's the type of listening that comes from

observing God's work in our lives. Now I don't believe every sneeze and hiccup is a sign from God. But I do believe if we ask for wisdom we can often see His hand and hear His voice in various circumstances.

There's another type of listening—the listening that involves observing God's awesome handiwork in creation. They say you really don't know an artist until you've seen his work. And there's probably no better way of learning of God's love than by drinking in the splendor of His creation. By creation we're not just talking pretty sunsets in the Bahamas. There's also the day-to-day creation of you—the new person you become as you dwell on the love and faithfulness He's shown to you in the past, or the goodness He's worked in other people's lives.

Finally, there is the type of listening that comes when we have quieted our soul enough to hear what Scripture calls that "still small voice"—that gentle nudging of the Holy Spirit as He softly guides and directs (see 1 Kings 19:11,12, *KJV*).

This is how we grow to understand God. By communicating with Him. By taking the time to talk and to listen. There is no other way to truly understand who He is. And, as we begin to understand who He is, there is no other choice we have but fall in love.

Day 4
An Understanding that Leads to Obedience

> *This is love for God: to obey his commands.*
> *And his commands are not burdensome, for*
> *everyone born of God overcomes the world.*
> 1 John 5:3,4

When my wife and I were first married there were dozens of things I did or didn't do that drove her crazy. But as I got to know her and fell more deeply in love with her I slowly changed. Not because I *had* to, but because I *wanted* to. As we drew closer and closer and I saw the pain and disappointment my shortcomings caused her, I did my best to change. Not for her—for me—for the satisfaction I experienced from pleasing her. Of course I'm still light-years from being the perfect husband but at least I'm heading in that direction. Not because I have to, but because I want to.

The same is true with sin and our relationship with Jesus. As we fall in love with Him, we slowly find that the areas of our disobedience begin to lose their appeal. Oh, we may still enjoy them, but experiencing the disappointment of our Greatest Love, or the momentary separation we feel from committing that sin, well, it's simply not worth the price of admission. We slowly find ourselves starting to change, to conform to Christ's image—not because we have to, but because we want to.

Now it's not always easy. Yes, there are times we have to bear down, using every ounce of self-control, fasting and praying for the strength to obey (or even the desire to obey). But the joy and satisfaction that obedience brings to our Lord and hence to ourselves, make it all worthwhile. So, as with everything else, we see that the key to understanding obedience lies in Jesus.

Obedience is not making up and following strict religious dos and don'ts. God desires relationships, not religion. He yearns for us, He woos us to become His Bride. He calls for us to become lovers, not legalists.

With that in mind there's only one way we can ever really understand and obtain lasting obedience. And it usually calls for very little effort on our part. All we have to do is allow ourselves to fall so deeply and totally in love with Jesus Christ that the obedience in our souls comes naturally—as naturally as falling into His arms.

Day 5
Understanding Ourselves

There is no fear in love. But perfect love drives out fear. 1 John 4:18

As we continue to look into understanding and Jesus' role in helping us truly understand, let's turn next to—ourselves.

I have a pet theory. It probably would never hold water in the scientific community but I definitely see it in my own life and I'm beginning to see it more and more in others. It's fairly simple and goes like this: My insecurities, my selfishness, my petty jealousies, my fears and worries, my mental stress, my failures with others, my self-hatred, my emotional turmoils, even my very sins come for one reason and one reason only—I simply do not know how loved I am.

How could I possibly worry over the details in my life if I really understood a love that knows the number of hairs on my head and cares for each one of them? (See Luke 12:7.)

How could I possibly be selfish if I really understood a love that will supply my every need?

How could I possibly be jealous, insecure and fearful around others if I really understood I was created for God's pleasure and that He is already delighting in me?

How could I be discouraged in my failures if God knows I'm but dust and still rejoices over me?

How could I possibly sin if I really understood that the dos and don'ts were created out of love for my well-being and that each intentional failure on my part pierces my Lover's heart?

Once again, the key to true understanding, (this time of ourselves) lies with Jesus. As we allow Him to scoop us into His arms and hold us tightly to His breast, our cares and shortcomings begin to fade. We begin to see ourselves as He sees us. Nothing, not even our own self-condemning natures, can touch us when we're held tightly in His arms.

The only way to understand that intense, all-consuming love is to understand the Lover. And, as we understand Christ, our view of ourselves changes. We begin to see ourselves through His eyes.

Perhaps that is what Jesus meant when He promised to give us His peace, a peace Paul described as "peace which transcends [exceeds] all understanding" (see John 14:27; also Phil. 4:7). Peace with God and, as our perceptions are conformed to His, peace with ourselves.

Day 6
Understanding Others

We love because he first loved us. 1 John 4:19

Before we leave this week's topic of Understanding, there's one other aspect we should explore.

Several years ago I was pulling into a parking space at the local supermarket when another car roared in from the wrong direction, cut me off and took the place. The scene is still vivid in my memory, not because of the driver's rudeness (hey, I live near L.A., I see rudeness every day) but because of my reaction. Instead of anger and outrage, I felt pity. For a few moments I was actually able to see the offender through Christ's eyes. And this is what I saw:

As far as the driver was concerned he was an orphan. He had nobody to look out for him. Anything he got he had to take. He did not know the loving Father in heaven who cared for him. He had to take and scrape and scratch and fight all on his own. I was moved with compassion for him, I was overcome with pity. (I wish I could react this way all the time but hey, I live near L.A., I see rudeness every day.)

However, for a few brief moment I was close enough to Christ's heart to see another human being as He sees him. And, instead of anger, I was moved with pity.

This sensitivity happens far too seldom in my life. But I do remember another time. A time when I was emotionally beat up and scathed by a Christian friend I was trying to help. Instead of anger and resentment I was again able to see him through Christ's eyes. This time I saw my friend as a precious animal hit by a car and left lying on the side of the road. If you've ever tried to help such an animal you know that your compassionate attempts can be met with vicious bites and attacks. Like an injured animal my friend was frightened, and he was in pain. He struck out at me—not because of anything I'd done and not because of anything he was—but because he was petrified, because he was scared to death. At that moment he simply did not have the assurance that he was really loved and cared for. At that moment he simply did not know how loved he was.

As you and I continue on our road to Emmaus and allow Christ to instruct us, we start to enter into true understanding. We start to understand God, Scripture, obedience, even ourselves. And finally, we start to understand others. We begin to see others as people in desperate need of that same relationship with Christ, that same all-encompassing love. We begin to understand that those who have hurt or offended us are not really the *offenders* but that they are really the *offended*. We begin to see that they are, not the enemy—but victims of the enemy.

And, as we begin to see that, we can't help but love them.

Footnotes

1. McDowell, Josh, quoting Peter W. Stoner in *Evidence That Demands a Verdict* (San Bernardino: Here's Life Publishers, 1979) p. 167.
2. Dylan, Bob, "When You Gonna Wake Up?" from the album *Slow Train Coming*, Colombia Records/CBS Inc., 1979.

2
REAL
RIGHTEOUSNESS

Day 1
Perfect Righteousness

*Mount Sinai was covered with smoke, because
the Lord descended on it in fire. The smoke
billowed up from it like smoke from a furnace,
the whole mountain trembled violently.*
Exodus 19:18

Because our finite minds can't comprehend the depth
of God's love, we tend to shorten the gap Jesus had to
bridge between us and the Father. We raise our position of
"goodness" just a touch and try to lower God's just a tad.
Not only does this mean we short-change God on His
glory but it also means we start to take our access to Him
for granted. We may almost flippantly approach His
throne, forgetting His awesome purity, His glory, His
perfect righteousness.

So, before we begin to look into Christ's work of
righteousness in our lives, let's remind ourselves exactly who
God is and the righteousness we must possess in order to
enter His presence.

For starters there was His terrifying presence on Mount
Sinai. A presence so pure that if the people so much as

touched the mountain they were to be executed (see Exod. 19:10-13).

Then there was the Ark of the Covenant, the gold and acacia wood container God instructed Moses to build for the Tabernacle. Because God's presence dwelt above the Ark, the object was so holy that once when a man reached out to steady it, to prevent it from falling to the ground, the Lord immediately struck that man dead (see 1 Chron. 13:7-10; also see Exod. 25:12-15).

Or how about the 70 men who were killed when they looked into the Ark? (See 1 Sam. 6:19.) The survivors knew exactly what they were talking about when they said, "Who can stand in the presence of the Lord, this holy God?" (1 Sam. 6:20).

Then there was the Lord's response when Moses, His faithful friend, pleaded to be able to see His glory: "You cannot see my face, for no one may see me and live" (Exod. 33:20).

And finally a New Testament passage describes God as the One "who alone is immortal and who lives in unapproachable light, whom no one has seen or can see" (1 Tim. 6:16).

This is the Holy God you and I are allowed to approach through Christ's blood. Awesome, terrifying and intensely pure. With this in mind maybe we can begin to appreciate the vast distance Christ's sacrifice bridged for us.

Day 2
False Righteousness

For it is by grace you have been saved, through faith—and this not from yourselves, it is the gift of God—not by works, so that no one can boast.
Ephesians 2:8-9

From the beginning of time we humans have tried to reach God (or a condition of godliness) through our own efforts, our own righteousness:

- from Adam and Eve whipping up some designer fig leaves to hide their nakedness,
- to Cain who did not bring his sacrifice in faith,
- to the people of Babel trying to build their way up to the heavens,
- to Muslims trying to work their way to God,
- to the Eastern religions who hope with enough tries they'll finally get it right (reincarnation),
- to the New Age folks who are trying to find it within themselves,
- to the multitude of Christians who are caught up in religious works for God instead of an intimate relationship with Him.

Why?

I guess it's the age-old problem of pride. After all, if we can reach God through our own righteousness, then we really don't need His help. And if we can reach Him on our own, doesn't that make us just a little bit like Him? Now there's a familiar lie: "For God knows that when you eat of it [the forbidden fruit] you will be like God" (Gen. 3:5).

The truth is, no matter how righteous we are, it's just not righteous enough—not enough to reach a God who's holiness makes mountains smoke and shake, who lives in "unapproachable light," who is so pure that scores are slain just by His presence. When comparing our righteousness with His, well there's not much comparison. It's little wonder then that the prophet cried, "All our righteous acts are like filthy rags" (Isa. 64:6).

So basically we're left hopeless, without any chance of ever approaching the all perfect, intensely pure God.

Well, at least not on our own...

Day 3
Temporary Righteousness

*Without the shedding of blood there is no
forgiveness.* Hebrews 9:22

From the beginning God required only one thing to make
us righteous. Only one thing can clean us up and wash us of our
sins: blood.

Cain was the first to find this out. Talk about a bad attitude! I
mean this guy tried to shortcut the blood sacrifice by sacrificing
"the fruits of the soil," instead of the firstborn of his family's
flock (see Gen. 4:3). God's response was basically a "No Sale."

But that was only the beginning. Throughout the Old
Testament the shedding of blood through animal sacrifice was
the primary way to obtain forgiveness.

It was the blood of a sheep or goat put over the doorways of
the children of Israel that protected them from the Angel of
Death in Egypt.

It was the blood of various animals that the priests used to
intercede for the people's sins. They sprinkled it in front of the
curtain of the sanctuary, put on the horns of the altar, at the
bottom of the altar, around the altar and on top the altar (see
Lev. 4—5). Moses even sprinkled blood on the people to confirm
their covenant with the Lord (see Exod. 24:8). In fact, the very
first priests were consecrated with blood on their clothes, their
right ear lobe, their thumb, and big toe (see Exod. 29:19-21).

Why? Why is God so interested in all this blood stuff? I
mean it sounds so sick and grotesque.

That's part of the reason. Sin is sick and grotesque. The
shedding of all this blood was to help remind us of the brutal
and ugly nature of sin. Sin conquers, it devours, it ravages. In
short, it destroys life. And instead of that destruction of life
falling upon the people, it was transferred to some innocent,
"unblemished" animal. Yes, it was ugly and brutal. But so is sin.

And yes, it probably disturbed God. But better the destruction of an innocent animal than the destruction of His people.

And why the emphasis on the actual blood?

What more accurately depicts the essence of a living life than its blood?

But there's another reason. And it is far more important than the others. All this brutality and bloodshed is nothing but a foreshadowing of the Great Sacrifice that would take place hundreds of years later. It is but a foreshadowing of the Final Sacrifice for all the world.

> *The blood of goats and bulls and the ashes of a heifer sprinkled on those who are ceremonially unclean sanctify them so that they are outwardly clean. How much more, then, will the blood of Christ, who through the eternal Spirit offered himself unblemished to God, cleanse our consciences from acts that lead to death, so that we may serve the living God!* Hebrews 9:13,14

> *Then he took the cup, gave thanks and offered it to them, saying, "Drink from it, all of you. This is my blood of the covenant, which is poured out for many for the forgiveness of sins."* Matthew 26:27,28

Day 4
The Cost of Our Righteousness

You were bought at a price. 1 Corinthians 7:23

The cost of bringing us up to God's standards of righteousness was incredibly high. It called for a blood sacrifice, alright—but more than just the blood of an animal or even more than the blood of a human. It called for God's blood. It called for the complete sacrifice of Jesus Christ—spiritually, emotionally and physically. To begin to really appreciate the cost He paid to make us righteous, let's take a brief look at the extent of that sacrifice.

Spiritual Sacrifice

Picture a perfect man who has never known sin, suddenly having to bear the sins of the world!

As little as I, being human, know God, the times I've been cut off from His presence have been nearly unbearable. Picture what the separation must have been like for Somebody who had always been present with the Father and who knew the Father perfectly, Somebody who knew the Father so well that the two were actually one! The separation experienced as God poured out all of His wrath for our sins on Jesus on the cross must have been a living hell! No wonder Jesus cried out, "My God, my God why have you forsaken me?" (Matt. 27:46).

Emotional Sacrifice

For a moment, try to feel the emotions Jesus must have suffered on the cross. Imagine being stripped naked and hung up high for all to see. Imagine the pain you feel seeing your friends' hopelessness—friends who had given up everything to follow you and who now wonder if it was all a sham. Imagine the pain you feel for your mother as she watches you being mocked and tortured. And, most importantly, imagine your heartbreak over a city you loved so much that you actually left your high position in heaven to come down and save, a city that has completely rejected that love, a city that in less than 40 years will be destroyed by their enemies for that rejection (see Luke 19:41-44).

Physical Sacrifice

And finally there is the physical anguish. It's interesting

to note that a great part of Christ's physical sacrifice is connected with blood—the blood the Old Testament emphasized as so necessary for making us righteous.

First Jesus sweat blood when He prayed in the Garden of Gethsemane (a medically proven condition known to happen to those undergoing the most excruciating emotional stress).

Then there was the crown of thorns (see Matt. 27:29). The crown was most likely constructed from local briars that have needle-sharp thorns that range from one to two inches in length. No doubt it was jammed down on top of His head—hard.

Then there was the flogging—beating with a whip (see John 19:1). The whip was made of several little whips, each with sharp, jagged rocks and shards of metal tied to their ends. These dug deeply into His back, filleting it beyond belief, shredding it beyond recognition.

And let's not forget the spikes driven through His hands and His feet.

And finally the piercing of His side with the sword so that blood and water spilled out (see John 19:34).

These are realities to dwell upon and to meditate over—not because of their morbid grotesqueness, but because they are proof of Christ's overwhelming love for us. They are proof of the awesome price He *wanted* to pay to make us righteous.

Day 5
The Privileges of Righteousness

You are a chosen people, a royal priesthood, a
holy nation, a people belonging to God.
1 Peter 2:9

Once we accept the righteousness Christ purchased for

us, the privileges and benefits are quite literally out of this world.

Forgiveness

Christ's sacrifice was so thorough and complete that believers are seen by God as being 100 percent pure and sinless. It makes no difference what we've done—it makes no difference how many impure thoughts we've had or how many people we've murdered. If we're truly repentant, our righteousness is absolutely perfect through Christ. "Though your sins are as scarlet, they shall be as white as snow" (Isa. 1:18)

Friendship with God

Because of our perfect righteousness, we now have access to the throne of the Creator of the universe. Any time day or night we may stand in the presence of a God so holy that, if it wasn't for our righteousness through Christ, we would simply keel over and die. But more than access, we have friendship and love—a love so deep that it can only be compared to the relationship of a loving Father and His child. But that's not all. We also have a special relationship with His Son—a relationship full of such compassion and commitment that it can only be described as the love a perfect Bridegroom has for His perfect Bride.

Heirship

> *To him who overcomes, I will give the right to sit with me on my throne, just as I overcame and sat down with my Father on his throne.*
> Revelation 3:21

Not only are you and I allowed access to God's throne, but according to this passage we are actually called to sit on that throne with Him. Because of the price Christ paid for us, you and I are now considered co-heirs with Him and are actually called to help Him rule!

Fruit of the Spirit

But there are more immediate benefits than ruling. Benefits we can enjoy today. Benefits such as having a piece of God, His very Spirit coming to live inside us.

Contrary to what New Agers teach, the presence of God inside us *does not* exist until our relationship with God is restored through Jesus. Only then does His Spirit breathe into ours, activating it, infusing it with His very presence, bringing it to life. And once we are brought to life, that "born again" spiritual life, we begin to experience living as He originally intended it.

> *The fruit of the Spirit is love, joy, peace,*
> *patience, kindness, goodness, faithfulness,*
> *gentleness and self-control.* Galatians 5:22,23

In short we are given the privilege of living the types of lives that God designed for us before sin entered our race—lives that, regardless of trials and testings, are overflowing and abundant.

These benefits are almost unfathomable—and they're all a result of the price Christ paid on the cross.

However, there's one other benefit that we sometimes overlook. A benefit we're all called to enjoy...

Day 6
All This Plus...

> *No one who is born of God will continue to sin,*
> *because God's seed remains in him; he cannot*
> *go on sinning, because he has been born of God.*
> 1 John 3:9

There's one other important benefit to accepting Christ's righteousness: *He works in us to perfect it.* That's right. With God's seed planted in our soul, His presence begins to take root and grow inside us. His presence begins choking out sin, loosening its strangle hold on us, and allowing us to actually become righteous. And the best news of all is it's not something we have to work up and labor over on our own. Righteousness starts to come to us naturally, as naturally as a fruit tree bears fruit (see Rom. 3:22).

Does that mean once we receive Christ that we'll never have to sin again? That's right. Will we sin again? Most likely.

It's true, sin's hold over us is broken once and for all, make no mistake about it: "Though you used to be slaves to sin...You have been set free" (Rom. 6:17,18). But it takes most of us a little while to really believe this, to really incorporate righteousness into our day-to-day lives. Paul probably put it best when he said:

> *Not that I have already obtained all this, or have already been made perfect, but I press on to take hold of that for which Christ Jesus took hold of me. Brothers, I do not consider myself yet to have taken hold of it. But one thing I do: Forgetting what is behind and straining toward what is ahead, I press on toward the goal to win the prize for which God has called me heavenward in Christ Jesus.* Philippians 3:12-14

We'll fall from time to time. Count on it. But the important thing is when we fall, we fall into the loving and forgiving arms of Jesus Christ. The important thing is that we allow Him to pick us up and help us continue on our road to right living.

I fully believe that there is no sin we cannot overcome. It won't always be easy. There may be plenty of failures, broken hearts and tears. Overcoming may take lots of fasting and prayer. But we do not have to go it alone. And eventually, if we *really* want (or even want to want) we will be freed from whatever sin is trapping and tormenting us.

> *The one who is in you is greater than the one* [Satan] *who is in the world.* 1 John 4:4.

> [Be] *confident of this, that he who began a good work in you will carry it on to completion until the day of Christ Jesus.* Philippians 1:6

3
COMPLETE REFUGE

Day 1
Noah's Ark

By faith Noah, when warned about things not yet seen, in holy fear built an ark to save his family. Hebrews 11:7

As we mentioned in chapter 1, the account of Noah and the ark is more than just an interesting historical event. It is also a wondrous picture of how Jesus Christ saves and protects His followers today.

God Instructs

For starters God told Noah what was going to happen and what Noah must do. Noah was not in the dark. He knew precisely what was coming down and precisely (to the very last cubit) what he must do to be saved.

The same is true with us. Scripture couldn't make it more clear about the judgment our groaning world will soon face. And Scripture couldn't make it more clear about what we must do to be saved.

But knowledge is only the first step. Hell will be full of people who had the knowledge of what to do. The next step is a little trickier, we have to...

Believe

Noah had to trust God. He had to trust Him enough to do the absurd. He had to trust God enough to build an ocean liner in the middle of a desert, to go out and collect a floating zoo and finally to climb inside and wait. This must have seemed like the weirdest, most foolish thing on earth to do to be saved.

And yet does it appear any more foolish than we Christians who put our hope in a poor, born-in-a-barn, vagabond miracle worker who hung out with bottom-of-the-rung riffraff until He underwent the most despised form of capital punishment known to man.

In both cases, the key element is faith—faith in God regardless of outward appearances. But faith is not the end. Next we have to...

Obey

According to Scripture, "Faith by itself, if it is not accompanied by action, is dead" (Jas. 2:17). If Noah had only believed God but not obeyed and stepped into that boat—well, he definitely would have gotten a chance to try out all of his swim strokes!

The same is true with us and Jesus. We have to actively put our trust in Him. Believing in Jesus isn't enough.

> *You believe that there is one God. Good! Even the demons believe that—and shudder.*
> James 2:19

We have to believe in Jesus enough to actually step on board and trust Him with our whole lives. We have to trust Jesus enough to let Him be both the Savior of our souls *and* the Lord of our lives.

And the result? As with Noah, we are completely saved from God's judgment as well as being saved from all the other storms the world tries to throw our way. Oh sure, the rain may pour, the wind may howl and the boat may do more than its fair share of rocking. But if we remain obedient, if we stay on board, we'll eventually come out the other end on safe and hollowed ground.

Day 2
Refuge from Day-to-Day Worries

You are my hiding place; you will protect me from trouble and surround me with songs of deliverance. Psalm 32:7

The little worldly cares are not something to shrug off and ignore. Granted, they're not in the same league as being hit by a Mack truck or discovering your daughter on the back of a milk carton. But they can be just as draining to your spiritual life. Jesus put it best in Luke 8 when He described worldly cares as weeds that grow up and slowly choke out the Word of God.

The strangling process may be slower and less obvious than major attacks, but it is just as effective. Nothing more thoroughly chokes off my spiritual life than the thousand and one day-to-day little pin pricks. Sure, I know God promises to be our protection and refuge in the big things. But somehow I get to thinking He's too big to help in the little things. I know that Jesus said, "Not a hair of your head will perish"(Luke 21:18), but what about the growing number of hairs I see each day in the drain after I shower? What about that Mastercard charge we can't seem to get off our bill? What about that subtle backbiter at school that keeps chomping away at my reputation? The erosion process may be slow, like the steady drip, drip, drip of a leaky faucet, but in the long run it can be devastating.

What can be done? In this war for our spiritual vitality (and it is a war), how can we fight an enemy that is barely noticeable?

We don't fight. We retreat. We seek refuge. We seek God's protective presence as surely as if we were under heavy attack.

How?

For me, I begin to quietly worship and praise. Often the quiet humming of a few favorite choruses does the trick. In heavier times of attack, slipping away for a slow thoughtful read of an appropriate psalm helps.

In either case I fully believe that the quickest way into God's protective presence is through praise. I'm sure that's what the psalmist meant when he said, "Enter his gates with thanksgiving and his courts with praise" (Ps. 100:4). There seems to be something supernatural about praise. Something that supernaturally transports me into His presence.

Now it's true, there are days I absolutely don't feel like worshiping. Days I feel like I'm being a hypocrite and think, *How can I possibly thank God when I don't feel the slightest bit thankful?*

But I found those are the days I need to praise God the most. So I force myself to thank Him—even through gritted teeth, even if it's only thanking Him for having teeth to grit. Regardless of how I feel, I press on. Praise is an act of my will not my emotions. The Bible specifically talks about "a sacrifice of praise" (Heb. 13:15). And sometimes that's exactly what my quiet songs are, a sacrifice.

But eventually, the Lord's peace and presence comes. Sometimes it takes longer than others—one, three, even five minutes. But eventually His truth and reality start to take hold and the world's attacks begin to appear for what they really are—a silly dripping faucet. And, a silly dripping faucet cannot possibly withstand the overwhelming flood of God's love.

Day 3
Refuge from Fear

> *An anxious heart weighs a man down.*
> Proverbs 12:25

Nothing steals my peace faster than fear. It is so false, such a lie, and yet I fall for it again and again—and again some more.

Fear is false because it contradicts what God says. Scripture is saturated with God's promises to protect and watch over the righteous. And even if He allows something bad to happen, He promises to use it for our good:

> *We know that in all things God works for the good of those who love him.* Romans 8:28

Yet part of me is always fearing that somehow some way God is going to take a nap, that He's going to let something slip past Him. It's such a lie. And yet, I'm so quick to buy into it.

It's little wonder then that Satan, described as "the father of lies" (John 8:44) uses this number one lie as a primary weapon in his arsenal to attack and wear me down.

So where's my defense?

Another description of Satan can be found in 1 Peter 5:8: "Your enemy the devil prowls around like a roaring lion looking for someone to devour." Interestingly enough, lions seldom roar when they're seriously stalking their prey. If they did that they'd always be scaring them off. No, in this case the roar is a blustering, false bravado kind of thing. It's basically just a lot of hot air to try and frighten us.

And that's the key. All Satan can do is try to frighten us. He can get in our faces with his best roar and try to scare us with all sorts of possible "what if" scenarios. He can do everything in his power to make us believe his roaring lies instead of God's quiet truth. He can do all of these things, but he can't touch us.

The trick is for us to decide who we really want to believe, who we really want to put our faith in: God or the liar. And, once we've decided upon God, we must fill our minds so full of His presence and promises that we drown out the liar's lies. Once again, I do this with quiet worshiping. Others read Scripture. Still others memorize verses. But whatever method we decide upon, the point is to keep our minds so full of God's promises that we can't hear the enemy's lies.

It's like Peter walking on the water (see Matt. 14:25-31). As long as we keep our eyes focused on Jesus and His promises, we'll do just fine. It's only when we start looking around in fear at the storm's wind and waves that we start to sink. But if we refuse to look at them, if we refuse to look at the lies and focus on God's truth, if we refuse to look at the "what ifs" of Satan and only look at the "I AM" of Jesus, we'll walk right over our deepest fears.

I'm not saying we won't get our hair a little mussed. But that's about all Satan's hot air can do—mess our hair a bit.

Day 4
Refuge from Worry

The truth will set you free. John 8:32

There's another way to seek refuge from the lies of fear and worry: Seek the truth.

The father of lies wields and manipulates fear beautifully. Somehow through his genius he is able to make fear feed upon itself in our minds until it has grown way out of proportion. Somehow fear feeds upon fear and grows to larger fear that continues to feed and grow, until we find ourselves running from a giant monster that has puffed itself up many times larger than reality.

As a result we begin to panic and palpitate over the *fear* of the situation instead of the actual situation—a neat trick and no doubt what was meant by the famous words of Franklin D. Roosevelt, "The only thing we have to fear is fear itself."[1]

So how do we fight this inflated monster? We face it down with truth. If there's a big threat hanging over your head take a good hard look at it. Ask yourself, *What is the worst that could possibly happen? What adjustments would I need to make if it did happen?* and *Could I live with those adjustments?* Play the whole scenario out in detail in your mind. By exposing the inflated fear to the actual reality, you'll discover that even the worst possibility is far less damaging than the fear of that possibility. As a result the fear begins to shrink to a manageable size. It begins to lose its icy grip over your heart and turns into something that you can handle.

Fear and worry make wonderful weapons in the arsenal of the father of lies. But the great thing about being a child of the God of Truth is that we can use His truth to unmask those lies. With the truth and promises of Jesus Christ we can approach that roaring lion of unmanageable fear and worry, unmask it and discover that it is nothing more than a pussy cat with a big mouth.

Day 5
Refuge from Self

For the sinful nature desires what is contrary to the Spirit, and the Spirit what is contrary to the

> *sinful nature. They are in conflict with each*
> *other, so that you do not do what you want.*
> Galatians 5:17

We've looked at how Jesus Christ provides refuge. Refuge from judgment, refuge from the cares of the world, refuge from the adversary and refuge from fear. But there's one other thing we need refuge from—ourselves.

As a Christian I often feel like a walking civil war. In my heart there is the constant battle between my old man (that has been genetically steeped in sin for thousands of years) and the brand new creature I've become through Jesus Christ.

To me the war appears to be fierce, the struggle intense. In fact, when Jesus talks about picking up our cross and following Him, I don't think of it in terms of the trials and persecutions of being a Christian. That's small potatoes (at least for most of us right now in western society). For me, the real cross is my flesh. The real cross is my old man, the part of me that wants to fight instead of forgive, that wants to swell with pride instead of bow in humility, that wants to take instead of give, that wants to doubt instead of believe. That's the heavy load of my old self that I must carry as I stagger and struggle towards Calvary.

It's interesting that one form of punishment in the Roman days involved tying the dead carcass of a human to the back of a living person. The poor person would have to carry this dead, decaying, putrefying carcass wherever he went for days and weeks—until he eventually collapsed from disease and emotional and physical exhaustion.

That's how I see myself—the good "Christian" part of me being dragged down by the other part—the lustful, fearful, insensitive, doubting, prideful, self-serving flesh. Those are the times I cry out to heaven with Paul, "What a wretched man I am! Who will rescue me from this body of death?"(Rom. 7:24).

Happily, the answer again lies with Christ, but not in a

way I can totally believe yet. You see, according to Scripture there is no war. That war was already won. Someone has already been to Calvary for us. My old nature has already been crucified. Technically, my old self is already dead:

> *For we know that our old self was crucified with him [Christ] so that the body of sin might be done away with that we should no longer be slaves to sin—because anyone who has died has been freed from sin.* Romans 6:6,7

> *You, however, are controlled not by the sinful nature but by the Spirit, if the Spirit of God lives in you.* Romans 8:9

If that's the case then the real war I'm fighting has nothing to do with the old man versus the new. According to Scripture that war has already been fought and won. The real war I'm fighting, as usual, comes down to my faith—whether I really want to believe that the old man is dead—whether I really want to believe that Christ has already won.

But, regardless of what battle I'm fighting—my imaginary "old man," or just my unbelief—I can still rest in the fact that, "there is now no condemnation for those who are in Christ Jesus" (Rom. 8:1). I can find peace in the fact that Jesus is at my side forgiving me, comforting me, helping me get back on my feet. I can rest assured that there is nothing I can do or not do, no failure in flesh or faith so great that it separates me from His love.

> *For I am convinced that neither death nor life, neither angels nor demons, neither the present nor the future, nor any powers, neither height nor depth, nor anything else in all creation, will be able to separate us from the love of God that is in Christ Jesus our Lord.* Romans 8:38,39

Day 6
Righteousness = Troublelessness

A righteous man may have many troubles,
but the Lord delivers him from them all.
Psalm 34:19

In our preaching of the gospel, we're not always as honest as we could be. Sometimes in our zeal we leave out the fine print. I mean, when is the last time you've heard an evangelist promise that if you become a Christian life will definitely be tough? Yet, that's certainly one of the promises Jesus made to us: "In this world you will have trouble" (John 16:33).

Somehow we've gotten it into our heads that being a Christian means smooth sailing, that God promises to always take us around the storms. And if He doesn't, we somehow feel betrayed. Or, if a brother or sister in the Lord is suffering we may even go so far as to question if there's "hidden sin" in his or her life.

Nothing could be further from the truth. The fact of the matter is that Jesus promises to protect us *within* the storm, to give us His peace *amidst* the troubles.

For obvious reasons, the persecuted Church behind the Iron, Bamboo and Koranic curtains has had a far better perspective of this truth. In fact for many of these folks there is a disappointment if they *can't* somehow suffer for Christ. In China one of the mottoes of earnest believers is "There is no crown without the cross."

But it doesn't stop in China. I've heard several stories of westerners assuring brothers and sisters in Eastern Europe that we are praying for them. But instead of showing thanks our persecuted brethren simply look down and sadly shake their heads. "No," they reply. "You've got it wrong. You're the ones in danger. You have no persecution. We are praying for *you!*"

Our brethren who have suffered know that our refuge in Christ comes from the peace He gives *inside* the storm. It is a supernatural peace that He gives us within our hearts, regardless of the outward circumstances.

With that in mind maybe the counsel of a good friend of mine isn't so far off. He suggests that whenever we go through the storms of life we should stop cowering in the hull. Since we're Christian and know God will protect us, we should stroll out onto the deck and enjoy the storm. We should experience the thrill of the wind and rain in our faces, marvel at the thundering and crashing waves. Oh we might get a little wet from time to time, but we'll be OK.

Maybe my friend's right. Maybe we should get out there and enjoy the drama and excitement of this show called "life." After all we do have His promises—and we do know how the final act will end.

Footnote

1. Franklin D. Roosevelt, from his First Inaugural Address, March 4, 1933.

4
THE DEPTHS OF REDEMPTION

He [Jesus] has become a high priest forever, in the order of Melchizedek. Hebrews 6:20

Another way of seeing Jesus in the Old Testament is to actually *see* Him. Many scholars think that we can literally see Christ in the Old Testament in the person of the mysterious high priest named Melchizedek. They believe this "mystery person" who appeared to Abraham back in Genesis was a "christophany": an actual physical appearance of Jesus Christ long before He was born in Bethlehem.

Here are just a few facts that lead to that conclusion:

- Melchizedek's name meant, "king of righteousness" (see Heb. 7:2). Jeremiah said that the Messiah would be called "The Lord Our Righteousness" (Jer. 23:6).
- He was king of Salem, which translated means "peace." So, in essence, he was the "king of peace" (see Heb. 7:2). Isaiah called the Messiah the "Prince of Peace" (Isa. 9:6).
- He appeared out of nowhere, "Without father or mother" (Heb. 7:3).
- He also was, "without beginning of days or end of life" (Heb. 7:3). Jesus said, "I am the Alpha and the Omega,

the First and the Last, the Beginning and the End" (Rev. 22:13).

- Whoever this guy was, he had more authority than Abraham because Melchizedek blessed Abraham. (In Old Testament times a lesser authority never blessed a higher authority.) Also, Abraham tithed 10 percent of his plunder to Melchizedek.
- And finally, to top it off, the writer of Hebrews describes Melchizedek as being "like the Son of God [remaining] a priest forever" (Heb. 7:3)

It's this final information that is the most interesting. Not only does the Bible say Melchizedek and Jesus are alike, but it refers to Melchizedek as a high priest *forever*.

Although not all Bible scholars would call Melchizedek a christophany (many consider him just a type or a foreshadowing of Jesus Christ), there is much to learn about his priesthood and how that office reached its pinnacle in Jesus. During the rest of this week we'll be examining how Jesus Christ still serves as that "forever" High Priest.

Day 2
Jesus: The True High Priest

The point of what we are saying is this: We do have such a high priest, who sat down at the right hand of the throne of the Majesty in heaven, and who serves in the sanctuary, the true tabernacle set up by the Lord, not by man.
Hebrews 8:1,2

When the writer of Hebrews referred to Jesus as our High Priest, it wasn't because he was running out of names to call Him. The truth of the matter is that no position or ministry better describes who Jesus is or what He did.

Ministry Similarities

In ancient Israel priests functioned primarily as the middlemen between God and His people, much as Jesus is the bridge between us and the Father. Like Jesus, the priests were the ones who could make acceptable sin offerings to God. They were the ones who taught the Word; they were the ones who blessed the people; they were the ones who offered intercessory prayers and they were the ones in some instances, who could declare the unclean as purified.

But the similarities go further than that. The Tabernacle in the desert and later the Temple in Jerusalem were built to the minutest detail according to God's exacting plans. And for good reason. They were a perfect symbol of the actual sanctuary in heaven (see Heb. 8:5). So, while the earthly priests served in shadowy symbolisms of heaven, our Heavenly Priest serves in the real thing.

Character Similarities

To compare Jesus Christ's character to the priests' is a joke. After all Jesus Christ was perfect and without sin. And yet, by the time the priests finished all of their ceremonial washings, dressings and blood sprinklings, they too were considered sinless—at least ceremonially.

It's also interesting to note that according to Leviticus 21, the priests had to be physically perfect and without blemish just as Jesus' character was perfect and without blemish of sin.

Now even though the High Priest may have been ceremonially sinless and without blemish, according to tradition, when he went into the sanctuary and behind the thick veil to enter God's presence, (something he could only do once a year), the other priests tied a rope around His ankle. That way if he dropped dead because he was unworthy of being in the presence of God's intense holiness, they could pull him out without going in there and being destroyed themselves.

But, as interesting as the similarities between the human priests and our Divine Priest are, they are only superficial shadows. Our Priest needs no ceremonial washings. Our Priest doesn't need to continually offer sacrifice after sacrifice to clean us from our sins. After all, those priests only used the blood of animals. Our Priest used *His* blood—the blood of the son of God. That blood is so potent and holy it only needed to be shed one time for all people (see Heb. 9:11-14,26).

Day 3
The Depth of Christ's Redemptive Love

> *The Lord said to me, "Go, show your love to*
> *your wife again, though she is loved by another*
> *and is an adulteress. Love her as the Lord loves*
> *the Israelites, though they turned to other gods."*
> Hosea 3:1

There are few stories that so clearly foreshadow the depth of Christ's redemptive love as our "forever" High Priest than the account of Hosea and Gomer.

Hosea was a prophet, a holy man of God who loved and obeyed His Lord. And yet God commanded Hosea to marry a prostitute named Gomer. How repulsive that must have been for a man who had spent his whole life striving for purity and holiness. Now this good, pure man must join himself with a prostitute, committing himself to being her faithful husband for the rest of his life. What a difficult task.

Yet how different was Hosea's task from the task Christ has performed for us? Christ's relationship to believers is pictured as a marriage (see Eph. 5:22-33). He has married us amidst our sins, our failures and our rebellion. The purest Man and most loving Being in the universe has selected us to become His Bride, to sit with Him on His throne. There was nothing we did to deserve it. There was only our sin, our rebellion—and His love.

But that's only half the story.

Even after Hosea and Gomer were married, even after Hosea had children with Gomer and remained a faithful and supporting husband, his wife ran off and began sleeping around with whomever could give her the finer things of life.

And what did God command Hosea to do? Stone her? Kill and destroy her as the Law says he had every right to do? No. He wasn't even allowed to hate and resent her. Instead Hosea was commanded to "love her as the Lord loves" (Hos. 3:1). The prophet, the renown man of God, went to the marketplace, endured whatever jokes and taunts that were hurled at him, and with a hefty price, bought Gomer off the auction block she had been placed upon (see Hos. 3:2).

What love. What commitment. And what a beautiful symbol of Christ's redemption.

Even though Jesus originally bought us for an incredible price, as Christians we still may stray. We still may be so attracted to the world and its pleasures that we start committing adultery with it—loving it more than Him. We may even allow sin and compromises to slip in until, before we know it, we've sold ourselves back into the slavery of sin.

But Jesus Christ remains faithful even when we are not. Because of the depth of His love, Jesus will search us out. He will make whatever sacrifice necessary to restore us and bring us back out of our slavery. And, once again, He will take us into His loving arms as His precious Bride. He will take us into His heart as His deepest, most treasured love.

Day 4
Christ's Commitment to Redemption

Suppose a woman has ten silver coins and loses one. Does she not light a lamp, sweep the house

> *and search carefully until she finds it? And*
> *when she finds it, she calls her friends and*
> *neighbors together and says, "Rejoice with me; I*
> *have found my lost coin." In the same way, I*
> *tell you, there is rejoicing in the presence of the*
> *angels of God over one sinner who repents.*
> Luke 15:8-10

Luke 15 recounts three parables Jesus told about redemption. It's as if Jesus is telling us that the concept of God's redemption is so large and multi-faceted, that it takes several illustrations to help our earthly minds grasp it. For the rest of this week we'll be looking into these parables of redemption and view other aspects of Christ's ministry as our High Priest.

All of the parables end with tremendous rejoicing and celebration when the person or object has been redeemed. That's how intense the Lord's love is for us. That's how important we are in His eyes. If just one of us turns from his sins and allows Christ to redeem him, all of heaven breaks into a celebration.

But the parable of the Lost Coin uncovers another unique aspect of Christ's redemption. Unlike the priests in the Old Testament or any other religious characters in any other religion, Jesus (represented by the widow) doesn't sit around and wait for us to find Him. Instead, He actively searches us out. We don't have to spend our lives staggering blindly about in search of some eternal truth, hoping against hope that somehow, someway, we'll stumble upon God. Jesus is already out there looking for us!

It was no small job this widow had before her—cleaning out the entire house, sweeping it, checking every inch with the light from her lamp. But she did not give up. She did everything in her power, she used every resource she had, until finally she found that one coin. Sure, she had other coins, but that one coin was so important to her, so precious, that she would not give up until she found it.

That is the kind of pursuing love our Lord has for us. He will do everything in His power to search for us, to find us, and to redeem us.

What a relief that is. What peace to know we don't have to run around reading every book we can find, buying every self-help tape on the market, investigating every religion-of-the-month. All we have to do is give up hiding and allow ourselves to be found.

Day 5
Christ's Method of Redemption

Suppose one of you has a hundred sheep and loses one of them. Does he not leave the ninety-nine in the open country and go after the lost sheep until he finds it? And when he finds it, he joyfully puts it on his shoulders and goes home. Luke 15:4-6

Sheep are stupid. They're stubborn. They're fearful. So the next time we read about Christ as the Shepherd and ourselves as the sheep, let's not think God is paying us any poetic compliments. Chances are He's just being honest.

In this parable we again see the commitment of the Great Shepherd as He goes out and searches for us. And we see the joy He experiences when we are found. But there's one unique aspect to this parable that sets it apart from the others. Not only does He seek us out, not only is He joyful when we're found, but He actually carries us. We don't even have to do that on our own. Jesus Christ will actually carry us into His abundant and eternal life!

This is a concept very different from the beliefs of worldly philosophies and religious systems. The following is a little illustration that may help clarify that difference:

Once there was a man so drunk that he stumbled out of a local party and fell into a deep cesspool. It was so steep and slimy that it was impossible to climb out. He was its prisoner. Desperately he cried for help. But no one heard. The nearby party was just too loud.

Eventually a wise teacher by the name of Buddha came upon the man.

"Can you help me?" the man cried.

"Certainly," Buddha replied. "Learn my wisdom, follow my teachings and you will be able to climb out." With that he turned and left.

The man tried his best to follow Buddha's advice but the walls were just too steep, their sides too slippery.

Next came Mohammed.

"Help me," the man cried.

"Certainly" Mohammed answered. "Simply follow God's rules and my commands and you will be free." With that Mohammed turned and moved on.

Desperately the man tried—again and again. And again and again he failed.

Finally a New Ager arrived.

"Please," the man cried, "you must help me!"

"Certainly," the person answered. "Just look deep within yourself and you'll discover you have the God-given strength to climb out." With that the New Ager also turned and left.

Once again the man tried his best, but to no avail. His efforts only made him more filthy and more depressed over his hopeless condition.

Finally Jesus appeared. "Do you want out?" He asked.

"Please sir," the man sobbed. "I'm trapped. I've tried everything. There's nothing more I can do."

"That's right," Jesus answered softly. And with that He climbed down into the stinking, slippery hole and carefully carried the man out.

That's the redemptive love of our Lord. Not only does

He search for us, not only does He rejoice when He finds us, but He actually wades into the filth of our sins, puts us on His shoulders, and carries us out.

Day 6
Christ's Redemptive Process

> *But while he was still a long way off, his father saw him and was filled with compassion for him; he ran to his son, threw his arms around him and kissed him.*
> *The son said to him, "Father, I have sinned against heaven and against you. I am no longer worthy to be called your son."*
> *But the father said to his servants, "Quick! Bring the best robe and put it on him. Put a ring on his finger and sandals on his feet. Bring the fattened calf and kill it. Let's have a feast and celebrate. For this son of mine was dead and is alive again; he was lost and is found."* Luke 15:20-24

The story of the lost son is one of the purest presentations of the process of Christ's redemption.

Free Will
At the beginning of the parable of the Lost Son, the father gave his son the inheritance and let him run off—much as God has given us free will to follow Him or run off and sin. The father knew what awaited his son in the world. He could have forbidden him from going out. He could have built a wall to stop him from leaving. But in the young man's eyes, that wall would not have been for protection. It would have been a prison. So, as painful as it was for the Father, he knew it was important to let his son go.

Enslavement of Sin

After blowing all of his money the young man wound up working and dining in a pigpen. (Only those who have worked around pigs can appreciate the filth and unique aromas of such a job. Also keep in mind that the kid was Jewish and pigs rated right at the top of the unclean list.)

The young man soon learned that sin is a baited hook. The same is true for us. A sin may look great on the outside, we may revel in it, satiate our senses with it, but eventually we'll find the hook. And subtly, without our even knowing it, that hook begins to pull us in. The sin has caught us. It is no longer serving us, we are serving it. We have become its slave.

Repentance

Eventually the lost son "came to his senses." He had learned what his father had known all along. The son returned to his father in great humility, admitting his sins and asking for forgiveness.

The Father's Response

Finally we see a father so excited and so full of love that he can't contain himself. Before his son even arrives, the man spots him, races down the road, throws his arms around his son, pig slop and all, and hugs and kisses him. This is a picture of the love Christ has for any who return to Him in repentance. It's not hesitant, it's not reserved. It's free-giving abandonment.

Summary

So, in looking back we can see that the parable of the Lost Son underlines the four basic steps of redemption:

1. Christ gives us free will and allows us to rebel.

2. We become enslaved and destroyed by our rebellion.

3. We finally "come to our senses"and repent of our rebellion.

4. And we wind back up in the Father's loving and forgiving arms.

5
CHRIST'S PROVISION

Day 1
Abraham and Isaac

When they reached the place God had told him about, Abraham built an altar there and arranged the wood on it. He bound his son Isaac and laid him on the altar, on top of the wood. Then he reached out his hand and took the knife to slay his son. But the angel of the Lord called out to him from heaven, "Abraham! Abraham!.... Do not lay a hand on the boy," he said.... "Now I know that you fear God, because you have not withheld from me your son, your only son."
Abraham looked up and there in a thicket he saw a ram caught by its horns. He went over and took the ram and sacrificed it as a burnt offering instead of his son. So Abraham called that place The Lord Will Provide. And to this day it is said, "On the mountain of the Lord it will be provided."
Genesis 22:9-14

No one warned me of the intensity of love I'd feel as a parent. No one told me about the moisture that would silently well up in my eyes when I held my little daughter, the lump that would catch in my throat when I see her overcoming life's little challenges, the rage when I watch her suffering from a fever or the heaviness in my chest as I look at her tiny ring finger and realize someday she will no longer be just mine.

The love of a parent for his or her child is indescribable, all-consuming. And yet, because the Lord commanded it, Abraham was willing to destroy the object of that love. The very thing Abraham treasured most God had asked him to sacrifice. What faith Abraham must have had. What commitment. What love.

But although the sacrifice of his only son had been required of Abraham, he didn't have to go through with it. Someone else would provide a sacrifice for him—first, through a ram, then centuries later, through the sacrifice of His own Son.

No human would be required by God to undergo the full agony and heartbreak of willfully destroying his own child. Only one Person in the universe would be required to undergo that type of hell, that tortuous grief.

And yet, how typical that is of our Lord—asking us to do difficult things and then stepping in and actually doing them Himself. What a loving, providing Father He is—insisting upon perfection from us, and then stepping in and being that perfection, Himself.

"The Lord Will Provide." As a loving Father he will provide anything that His children need, from day-to-day trifles to our salvation. No sacrifice is too great for such a loving Father, no provision too small.

"The Lord Will Provide." What a perfect name for Abraham to give that mountain. What's more perfect still is that many historians and archaeologists believe it was on this very mountain that God's greatest provision took place. Many scholars believe that it was on this exact mountain, centuries later, that God sacrificed His own Son, making the ultimate provision—the provision of eternal life.

Day 2
Material Provision

*Therefore I tell you, do not worry about your life,
what you will eat or drink; or about your body,
what you will wear. Is not life more important
than food, and the body more important than
clothes? Look at the birds of the air; they do not
sow or reap or store away in barns, and yet your
heavenly Father feeds them. Are you not much
more valuable than they? Who of you by
worrying can add a single hour to his life?*

*And why do you worry about clothes? See
how the lilies of the field grow. They do not
labor or spin. Yet I tell you that not even
Solomon in all his splendor was dressed like one
of these. If that is how God clothes the grass of
the field, which is here today and tomorrow is
thrown into the fire, will he not much more
clothe you, O you of little faith?*
Matthew 6:25-30

I wish I would take these verses more seriously. I wish I would really believe that Jesus will always take care of my house payments, my taxes, my medical insurance, and yes, that He'll even clothe my wife and daughter!

I wish I would take these verses more seriously. I wish I totally relied on the fact that Christ will provide my every need. Actually He promises more than that. He promises to meet all my needs with greater splendor than that of Solomon, one of the wealthiest men who ever lived!

Why do I fight and argue to prove that Scripture is 100 percent accurate and yet refuse to take these verses as 100 percent truth? Why do I pore over Jesus' every word and accept them as fact but treat this passage as if He was just taking poetic license? I trust Jesus Christ with my eternal soul, why won't I trust him with a $600 house payment?

Jesus had the answer when He described people like me in the end section as "you of little faith."

That's the key: faith.

God's provision is there. It's simply a question of whether I want to believe Him or not. Do I really want to focus my eyes on Christ and start walking in faith? Do I really want to refuse to look at the roaring wind of inflation, the churning waters of IRS hassles, the crashing waves of oh-no-the-Social-Security-System-is-going-down-the-drain-what-am-I-going-to-do-for-retirement?

That is the ultimate question. Do I really want to lock my sights onto Jesus, trusting His promises and walking above my day-to-day financial worries? Or would I prefer to spend the rest of my life fighting and fretting for what He's already promised to give me?

When I look at the choices, it's not a tough decision. But, as always, it's up to me.

Day 3
All Things Given

So do not worry, saying, "What shall we eat?" or "What shall we drink?" or "What shall we wear?" For the pagans run after all these things, and your heavenly Father knows that you need them. But seek first his kingdom and his righteousness, and all these things will be given to you as well. Matthew 6:31-33

The world's worries constantly scream at me. They are a continual roar in my ears in the heat of my day-to-day battles over making a living, or studying for exams, or office politics, or fighting about who's going to pick up the kids. I mean, let's face it, I'm lucky if I can even *hear* that "still small voice" let alone *obey* it!

"Just don't worry," you say? Those are pretty easy words. But what do you do when Reality says otherwise. What do you do when Reality says "If you don't get out there and fight and scrap and kick with everybody else to get what you got to get, it ain't going to be gotten!"?

One of the things you can do is remember God's faithfulness in the past...

When I was a little guy in Seattle, I lived for Sea Fair Days. It was a time of picnics, boat rides, celebrations, hydroplane races and the big, *Sea Fair Parade!*

One time we arrived at the parade route early enough to find a perfect place on the curb. The parade unfolded right before us. I watched with saucer-like eyes as the glittering floats passed, the marching bands marched and the prancing horses pranced.

Then it came—the Sea Fair Float with the Sea Fair Pirates! They tossed candy onto the street and everyone laughed as the kids scrambled out screaming and fighting for as much candy as their greedy little hands could grab. The float came closer and closer.

I thought, *This is going to be great. The next handful should land in the street right in front of me!*

But just before the float arrived, just before it was my turn to race out, my mom leaned over and said, "I don't want you to run out there. I want you to stay here on the curb."

I was heartbroken, devastated. But I quietly obeyed and watched as all the kids around me leaped out into the street to fight and scrap and kick for a piece of candy. It made no sense to me and it was tough. But I obeyed.

And then, high atop the float, the Captain of the Pirates saw what was happening. Without a word He climbed down, hopped off the float and headed directly toward me. I was frightened and thrilled at the same time. He hovered over me for just a second. Then he smiled, said something I couldn't understand and in front of everyone, he dumped the biggest handful of candy I had ever seen right into my lap.

I have never forgotten that experience. I did not have to get out into the street to fight and scrap and kick. All I had to do was obey. Even when it didn't make sense. All I had to do was sit and obey. As a result I received more than anyone would have dreamed.

In a way this story illustrates what Jesus was talking about in Matthew 6. As I seek God first, as I focus upon Him, obey Him and seek His righteousness, He will always provide—abundantly.

Day 4
Provision of Peace

Peace I leave with you; my peace I give you. I do not give to you as the world gives.
John 14:27

Awhile back when I was first starting this treacherous course called "adulthood," I spent the day working at a famous millionaire's ranch. He had everything and then some. He also had pretty good eyesight and noticed me ogling and drooling over his empire.

Later that afternoon he strolled over to our pickup and said, "Son, you ain't gonna believe what I'm gonna say but I gotta say it anyways. You see all this stuff?"

"Yes Sir," I stuttered, doing my best not to salivate all over his thousand dollar suit and real alligator boots.

"You won't believe this," he repeated, "But I was happier when I was poor like you than I have been since I got all this here money. Now all I worry about is who's gonna try and steal it from me and how they're gonna try and do it."

He was right. I didn't believe him—at least not for a while. But over the years as I've watched my baby boomer buddies buy their bigger homes, their bigger screen TVs and their bigger BMWs, I've noticed something. I've noticed that the more they've tried to buy peace and contentment, the more it has eluded them.

Sure, they're all smiles and good times on the outside. Who wouldn't be with their spas, their gorgeous children and their condos in Colorado. And sure, I'm usually jealous—at least for a while. But when I spend the time to really talk and listen to my "successful" friends, it doesn't take long to discover that these beautiful people with their beautiful lives are riddled with intense fears, depression and emptiness.

And for good reason. They are desperately trying to buy a peace and fulfillment that they cannot buy. They are desperately seeking a peace from the world that the world cannot give—peace with themselves, peace with their lives and above all, peace with God.

As Christians, you and I don't have to fall into that vicious cycle of earning more money to buy more things to try to buy peace. If we honestly put our trust in Christ, we can cut out the first two steps of making more bucks to buy more things. Instead, we can go directly to the Source of peace and receive it—no matter what our outward circumstances may be.

I've just returned from a trip to China, visiting members of unofficial home churches. These rural peasants are some of the poorest and most persecuted Christians I have ever met. They are also the happiest and most content. Why? Because of their reliance on the Author and Finisher of peace. For it was He who said, "Peace I leave with you; my peace I give you. I do not give to you as the world gives. Do not let your hearts be troubled and do not be afraid" (John 14:27).

Day 5
Provision of Life

I have come that they may have life, and have it to the full. John 10:10

Perhaps all of God's provisions can be summed up into this one promise—LIFE—life as Christ had originally designed it, life that is full, abundant, overflowing. And that's just for beginners! That's just for those who have asked Him to forgive their sins and be their Lord!

Those who are serious about really getting down and serving with Him soon discover a deeper principle. They discover that it's absolutely impossible to out-give God. The more they give of their lives to serve Him, the more He gives of His life back to them. It's a wonderful "nonvicious" cycle. We give, He gives more. We give more from what He has given us, and He gives even more.

That doesn't mean everything's always roses—on the contrary. But, if we are serious about serving Christ, He is serious about blessing and supporting us.

As a teenager I promised the Lord that I would go into full-time service for Him when I turned 20. Little did I know that on my 20th birthday I was in the middle of the Israeli wilderness with dysentery. *Hmm,* I thought, *so this is what I have to look forward to.*

But from that time on my life has never been the same. Yes it has been full of sacrifice and occasional lean times, but not once have I given of my life and time that it has not returned, multiplied many times over.

My Yuppie friends with all of their Yuppie toys look at the fullness of my life and shake their heads in amazement. I have never devoted my life to making money, seeking pleasures or worldly adventures. And yet my life, with writing books, directing films, traveling all over the world, beautiful family, home, and above all, with the eternal qualities God is instilling in me—well it just leaves my friends in awe.

Come to think of it, it does me, too. I haven't been so blessed because I'm such a great person. (My friends and family can attest to that.) And it's not because I have sought any of these things on my own. But because I've devoted my life, with all of its faults and frailties, to serving Christ. And as a result of that service, the past 15 years of my life have been richer and fuller than I could have ever possibly imagined.

So, if you hear even the slightest inner whisperings about full- or part-time service to the Lord, listen carefully. It may be the Holy Spirit asking if you're interested in embarking on the most incredible and adventurous journey imaginable. It may not always be easy, but it will always be full and overflowing. It will always be abundant with—LIFE.

Day 6
The Key to Receiving Christ's Provisions

For it is by grace you have been saved, through faith—and this not from yourselves, it is the gift of God. Ephesians 2:8

There are many other areas of provision that Christ supplies in our lives: holiness, good works, love, patience, joy, perseverance. You name it, if it's for our best, He'll supply it.

Why? There are two reasons.

First, Christ loves us so much that He wants us "mature and complete, not lacking anything" (Jas. 1:4). He wants us to experience the joy of functioning as He had originally designed us.

He knows we can't function according to His original design on our own—not anymore. We're too crippled. There's been too much sin in our past. Just as it is with our salvation, so it is with every other good thing in our lives. God must do the work.

You may think, *But we have to do something!*

And you are right, we do. We have to have faith. We have to believe Him and be willing to receive His provisions. We are like men and women dying of thirst in the desert. Suddenly Jesus Christ appears. In His hand is a pitcher of cool, pure water. He gave His life to purchase this precious, life-giving water. And now He will do anything He can to help us drink it. He will even pour it into our mouths. All we have to do is have enough faith to open our mouths. That's it. He will do the rest.

"But," you say, "what if I don't even have that much faith? What if I don't believe He'll supply my financial needs, my emotional needs? What if I don't believe He will give me peace? What if I doubt that He can fix all my 'incompleteness' and make me whole? In short, what if I don't even have the faith to open my mouth to receive that water?"

That's a good question. But here's an even better answer:

Dwell with Him. Look into Christ's eyes. Through quiet communing with Him in prayer and reading of His Word, you will discover His reality becoming more real than the reality you're fighting. Gradually as you look to Christ, you will find yourself miraculously receiving His faith to overcome your doubt.

Why? Because He knows we're not even strong enough to have faith on our own. I'm afraid we even have to turn to Jesus for that. This is what the writer of Hebrews meant when He said, "Let us fix our eyes on Jesus, the author and perfecter of our faith" (Heb. 12:2). He is the source of our faith. Not us, Him.

Yes, faith is the key. Absolutely. We must have the faith to receive His provisions. But like everything else, we can't even do that on our own.

With this cold, hard fact in mind, one of my favorite Bible passages and one that gives me the most comfort is in the Gospel of Mark:

Jesus asked the boy's father, "How long has he been like this?"

"From childhood," he answered. "It [the demon possessing his son] has often thrown him into fire or water to kill him. But if you can do anything, take pity on us and help us."

"'If you can'?" said Jesus. "Everything is possible for him who believes."

Immediately the boy's father exclaimed, "I do believe; help me overcome my unbelief!"
Mark 9:21-24

With that, Jesus turned and cast out the demon, completely curing the boy.

All things are possible with God—even the faith to make those things possible.

6
THE DEMAND
FOR OBEDIENCE

Day 1
Joseph: A Type of Christ

*Joseph said to his brothers..."God sent me
ahead of you to preserve for you a remnant on
earth and to save your lives by a great
deliverance."* Genesis 45:4,7

When it comes to Old Testament lives, there are few who
typify the obedience of Jesus Christ more closely than Joseph. I
mean this poor guy went through everything in the book and
then some. And yet, no matter how dark things looked, he
remained obedient to God. No matter how "unfaithful" God may
have appeared on the surface, Joseph hung in there, trusting and
obeying Him, foreshadowing the obedience of Jesus many
centuries later.

Early on in his life, God revealed to Joseph in a dream that he
would be a major, big-time ruler. Although this promise was made
to a mortal about an earthly kingdom, it parallels the promise the
Father made about His own Son.

So Joseph was going to be a king. That was the good news.
The bad news was he'd have to wait a few decades for it to happen.

When he was still a teenager, Joseph was betrayed and
sold into slavery by his jealous brothers for 20 pieces of silver.

In much the same way, Jesus was betrayed by his "brother" for 30 pieces of silver.

But instead of grumbling and turning his back on God, Joseph grew where he was planted, in the household of an Egyptian. Joseph remained faithful to God and God blessed him. Eventually he was put in charge of his master's entire household. (It's interesting that once again the Lord didn't remove one of His children from a difficult situation. Instead, He blessed him in the middle of it.)

But the trials weren't over yet. It was because of Joseph's faithfulness and obedience (by refusing to go to bed with the boss's wife) that he found himself unjustly thrown into prison. I don't know about you, but by about that time I would have started whining a few choruses of "Why Me God?" I might have even been tempted to chuck all of this "faithfulness stuff." I mean, where was it getting me?

But not Joseph. Once again he remained obedient and faithful. And, amidst the difficulties, God again blessed him. He became head of all the prisoners. Then, to top it off, one of his good buddies was getting out on parole. This buddy was so impressed with Joseph's ability to interpret dreams that he promised to put in a good word for him to the king. Now at last, things seemed to be turning out as God promised.

Well, not exactly...

As good buddies are prone to do, this one let Joseph down. By now I would have been seething with anger and resentment. I mean, what does a righteous saint of God have to do to get a little recognition, anyway!?

But not Joseph. He still remained faithful. He still trusted God. And eventually, through no manipulation of his own, but by remaining faithful, Joseph rose to take charge of all of Egypt—the most powerful nation in the world!

Because of Joseph's obedience, regardless of the cost, God's promise to him was fulfilled. He became a type of ruler/savior—much as Jesus is Lord and Savior through His persistent obedience.

But Joseph, like Jesus, did not become ruler for his own glory. Both used their power and authority to serve and deliver others. In fact, Joseph used his position to bring about reconciliation to the very brothers who had betrayed him. He also saved their lives by providing them with food during a great famine. In all of this, Joseph saw God's will at work and probably put it best when he said, "God sent me ahead of you to preserve for you a remnant on earth and to save your lives by a great deliverance" (Gen. 45:7).

Day 2
No Option

I know your deeds, that you are neither cold nor hot. I wish you were either one or the other! So, because you are lukewarm—neither hot nor cold—I am about to spit you out of my mouth.
Revelation 3:15,16

In this age of "cheap grace" and "convenient Christianity," it's far too easy to look upon obedience as an option—as something I'll do if I get around to it—something I'll do on my schedule, at my leisure, if it doesn't put me out.

But to God obedience is not an option. It is a command: "Be perfect, therefore, as your heavenly Father is perfect" (Matt. 5:48).

Cheap Grace may say, "Hey, I'm a Christian, I'm saved. I usually try to follow God's commands. If I do, great. If I don't, no biggie. I mean, after all, the Bible says, 'There is now no condemnation for those who are in Christ Jesus'" (Rom. 8:1).

That's true. But I can't help thinking that for all of us who use and abuse Christ's grace, like it's some sort of unlimited credit card for sin—I can't help wondering if someday our credit will run out.

Cheap Grace argues, "Come off it, I believe in Christ. That's all that counts."

The answer to that argument is both yes and no.

James said, "You believe that there is one God. Good! Even the demons believe that—and shudder" (Jas. 2:19).

You see, the belief referred to in Scripture is intended to be more than a mental nod. It is meant to be a *life-changing* belief. But even if people only get by with enough "fire insurance" belief to save them from the flames of hell, think of the blessings and joys they miss by sidestepping God's fullest will in their lives. I'm a firm believer that every time we take God's hand in obedience, there is a hidden blessing in His palm.

Even if that wasn't the case, what a miserable relationship that must be with Christ—to think that they're simply conning Him, that they're using Him like some Kleenex to blow their noses in and then throw away at their convenience.

There's something so cleansing, so freeing when we stand before Christ knowing we've sincerely tried and sincerely failed. But there's something so dirty and cheap in standing before Him knowing we've used Him. Yes, we may be forgiven. Yes, His blood has covered our sins. But what becomes of our relationship with Christ—that intimacy that's so important for us to have?

All this to say, Scripture implies that we may be called upon to resist "to the point of shedding your blood" (Heb. 12:4). How sad it is for us when we simply resist to the point of inconvenience.

Day 3
Principles of Obedience

To obey is better than sacrifice. 1 Samuel 15:22

There are certain promises God has made in Scripture

regarding this present life concerning obedience and disobedience. Here's just one section:

> *If you fully obey the Lord your God and carefully follow all his commands I give you today, the Lord your God will set you high above all the nations on earth. All these blessings will come upon you and accompany you if you obey the Lord your God:*

> *You will be blessed in the city and blessed in the country.*
>
> *The fruit of your womb will be blessed, and the crops of your land and the young of your livestock—the calves of your herds and the lambs of your flocks.*
>
> *Your basket and your kneading trough will be blessed.*
>
> *You will be blessed when you come in and blessed when you go out.*
>
> *The Lord will grant that the enemies who rise up against you will be defeated before you. They will come at you from one direction but flee from you in seven.*
>
> *The Lord will send a blessing on your barns and on everything you put your hand to. The Lord your God will bless you in the land he is giving you.*
>
> *The Lord will establish you as his holy people, as he promised you on oath....All the peoples on earth will see that you are called by the name of the Lord, and they will fear you. The Lord will grant you abundant prosperity—in the fruit of your womb, the*

young of your livestock and the crops of your ground—in the land he swore to your forefathers to give you.

The Lord will open the heavens, the storehouse of his bounty, to send rain on your land in season and to bless all the work of your hands. You will lend to many nations but will borrow from none. The Lord will make you the head, not the tail. If you pay attention to the commands of the Lord your God that I give you this day and carefully follow them, you will always be at the top, never at the bottom. Do not turn aside from any of the commands I give you today, to the right or to the left, following other gods and serving them.

However, if you do not obey the Lord your God and do not carefully follow all his commands and decrees I am giving you today, all these curses will come upon you and overtake you:

You will be cursed in the city and cursed in the country.

Your basket and your kneading trough will be cursed.

The fruit of your womb will be cursed, and the crops of your land, and the calves of your herds and the lambs of your flocks.

You will be cursed when you come in and cursed when you go out.

Deuteronomy 28:1-19

The curses for disobedience continue for the next 48 verses! All this to say, it sounds like obedience is fairly important to God.

Lord, may it become more important to me.

Day 4
The Power of Obedience

You are my friends if you do what I command.
I no longer call you servants, because a servant
does not know his master's business. Instead,
I have called you friends, for everything that
I learned from my Father I have made known
to you. You did not choose me, but I chose
you and appointed you to go and bear
fruit—fruit that will last. Then the Father
will give you whatever you ask in my name.
John 15:14-16

If you're a theologian you might not want to read today's section. I can't create an ironclad case with Scripture for what I'm about to say. And, since it's based more on experience than Scripture, it needs to be taken with a couple pounds of salt. But I would like to share what has proven to be a reality—at least in my life.

When I seriously wrestle and strive for obedience, my communication lines with the Lord are clearer and my prayers more potent. At first I thought this was just a coincidence, but it's proven to be a recurring pattern. The first time it really struck me was a few Christmases back. There was this one "tiny" area of blatant disobedience in my life. For years I knew I should take care of it but I just didn't get around to it. Then for one reason or another I decided it was time. And almost immediately my prayers seemed to take on a deeper potency. It seemed everything I prayed about was answered as soon as I prayed about it! Everything from finding impossible to find books in stores, to parking places, to a healed relationship, to one of the most exciting job openings in my career as a filmmaker.

But for me the real topper came when I was at the All School Christmas pageant. My three-year-old was up in the chorus singing something real spiritual about reindeer or Santa Claus or something. There was this older kid standing in front of her with giant cutout antlers the size of Cleveland on her head, which managed to block out any sign of my daughter's existence. Not a good situation for an anxious dad with camera in hand.

But, recalling how successful my prayer life had been the past few days, I wondered if I should bother God with such a trifling request. Then, almost as a type of experiment, I went ahead. I asked the Lord to get rid of that kid in front so I can get my photo. And no less than 10 seconds after that holy and contrite prayer, the little girl with the big antlers suddenly broke out in tears and dashed off the stage. I was dumbstruck. Amazed. And more than a little guilty (although I did manage to fire off a few good shots).

Is an experience like that something to build an entire theology on? Absolutely not. Were my motives entirely pure? Wrong again. Was it in God's perfect will? I doubt it. But time and time again it seems that the more serious I am about honoring the Lord in obedience, the more serious He is about honoring my requests.

You may be thinking, *But aren't you saying you're putting your faith in your works instead of in Jesus Christ? After all it was your works that supposedly got your prayers answered.*

No. My motivation for obedience is to draw closer to the heart of my Lord—that's where my faith lies. I am not trusting in obedience to do anything, let alone manipulate Christ into getting my way. What Jesus does after I obey is up to Him. What I am saying is that the closer I draw to Christ through obedience, the more sensitive I become to my Friend—and the more sensitively my Friend responds to me.

Day 5
Heroes

*Do not merely listen to the word, and so deceive
yourselves. Do what it says....The man who
looks intently into the perfect law that gives
freedom, and continues to do this, not forgetting
what he has heard, but doing it—he will be
blessed in what he does.* James 1:22,25

It seems that all of the great heroes of the Bible had one thing in common: obedience. Yes, they all had faith, but the real great ones were willing to put that faith into action through obedience. Let's take a look at just a couple of these heroes, noting what God required of them, how they obeyed and how God blessed them for that obedience.

Abraham

We've already examined Abraham and his great obedience in preparing to sacrifice his son. It's interesting that God didn't just ask Abraham if he was willing to sacrifice Isaac. The Lord required him to go through with much of it: the long walk to the location, the preparation of the altar, the tying of Isaac to the altar, even the actual raising of the knife. This was no test of theoretical faith Abraham was going through. This was a test of obedience.

And the Lord's response to Abraham's obedience?

*I swear by myself, declares the Lord, that
because you have done this and have not
withheld your son, your only son, I will surely
bless you and make your descendants as
numerous as the stars in the sky and as the
sand on the seashore. Your descendants will
take possession of the cities of their enemies,*

and through your offspring all nations on earth
will be blessed, because you have obeyed me.
Genesis 22:15-18

Gideon

Gideon was a wimp—the weakest member of the weakest family in a nation so weak that its people were hiding out in caves. In short, Gideon was as low on the macho scale as you can get. Yet, through his obedience—first with smaller things (like tearing down his father's altar) and then larger (like reducing a 10,000 man army to 300 and then attacking the enemy by shouting, blowing trumpets, and smashing pottery), he became a hero.

Gideon obeyed. Sure, he had his doubts and needed a little coaching from time to time, but this only proves that God will always help us, even in our weaknesses.

And the results of Gideon's obedience? His nation was safe from the invasion of the Midianites and the people turned to this number one loser and begged him to:

Rule over us—you, your son and your
grandson—because you have saved us out of the
hand of Midian.
But Gideon told them, "I will not rule over you,
nor will my son rule over you. The Lord will rule
over you." Judges 8:22,23

Day 6
What If...

Whoever serves me must follow me; and where
I am, my servant also will be. My Father will
honor the one who serves me. John 12:26

In one sense the life of the great preacher and teacher, D.L. Moody could be looked upon as a vast experiment. He wanted to find out what would happen if a man simply said yes to God for an entire lifetime. And since there were no volunteers to pick from, Moody chose himself for the experiment.

The result? One of the greatest evangelists and ministries ever to be birthed in America. A ministry that literally changed the world.

What would happen today if each of us were to take obedience as seriously as that—as seriously as God takes it? What would happen if obedience became our number one priority—above our work, our schooling, even above our families? What would happen if we purposed in our hearts to say yes to Jesus regardless of the cost?

We'd definitely be able to change the world. If one wimpy Gideon could change a nation, imagine what a thousand, ten thousand of us wimpy little Gideons could do for a world?

And, to top it off, we'd definitely be experiencing the abundant life Jesus promised. Maybe not abundance as far as things, but abundance as far as cutting edge, overflowing, exciting life. Who knows, maybe we wouldn't even have to dump 20 bucks at an amusement park to get a little thrill or spend six dollars at a movie theater for a little make-believe excitement. Instead, we'd actually be living that excitement!

The trick is to look past the short-term comforts and pleasures that disobedience promises. The trick is to look past the common sense, here-and-now solutions disobedience insists upon. It may not always be pleasant. It was no picnic for Jesus, Joseph, Abraham, Gideon or even Moody. But each of them refused to look at the present circumstances staring them in the face. Instead, they forced themselves to see beyond—beyond to where God's great promises and faithfulness would eventually be fulfilled.

Obedience. What masterpieces the Lord could paint if

He only had brushes that would respond to every move of His hand. What lives could be changed by souls willing to do whatever He asked. What life our sick and dying world could receive if there were just enough of us willing to obey.

Dear Lord, raise us up, make us willing to become men and women who simply and always say yes.

7
TIME TO
REMEMBER

For Christ, our Passover lamb, has been sacrificed.
1 Corinthians 5:7

Our Lord seems to put an emphasis on symbols and traditions. It's as if He knows our memory of His love is so feeble that we need all the reminders we can get. But in our zeal to keep Christianity fresh and alive I wonder if we modern day Christians sometimes fail to give the proper importance to these reminders.

For this week let's explore just a few of the Bible's symbols and traditions with the hope that they'll make Christ a little more fresh and alive to us.

One of our first and most cherished traditions is Communion or the Lord's Supper. Here we personally receive His sacrifice for ourselves by symbolically eating His broken body and drinking His cleansing blood. But the symbolism of this meal began long before Christ's Last Supper with His disciples. It started more than 1400 years earlier. For 1400 years the Jews had been eating and celebrating this meal (called Passover) as a reminder of how God had delivered them out of Egypt. Then Jesus came on the scene and gave the meal a new and deeper meaning. He actually insisted that the food really pointed to Himself! To see Jesus' point more clearly, let's take a quick look at some of the basic elements of the Passover meal.

Bitter Herbs

First of all there was the eating of bitter herbs, delectable delicacies of snake root, dandelions, lettuce and peppermint. Yum. The bitter herbs were to remind the Israelites of the bitterness of their bondage to Egypt. Today they could serve as a strong reminder of the bitterness of our bondage to sin.

Passover Lamb

Next there was the lamb. We've briefly discussed how Jesus is the Lamb of God who takes away our sins. But just in case there are any doubts, here are a few other similarities between the Passover lamb and the Lamb of God:

- The Passover lamb had to be unblemished, just as Jesus was unblemished (without sin). (See Exod. 12:5; 1 Pet. 2:22.)
- The Passover lamb was to have no broken bones, just as Jesus' bones were not broken on the cross. (See Exod. 12:46; John 19:33-36.)
- The lamb had to be completely roasted in fire, just as Jesus had to completely undergo the wrath (frequently symbolized by fire) of the Father. (See Exod. 12:9; 1 Pet. 2:24).
- The lamb had to be totally eaten, just as we have to totally "consume" Jesus. Christ allows no partial salvation or partial Lordship; it's all or nothing. (See Exod. 12:10; John 14:21-24.)

Unleavened Bread

In the Bible leaven (yeast) often represents sin. In the Passover eating bread without leaven represents the haste with which the Israelites left Egypt. (They did not even have time to wait for their bread to rise!) So today the bread of communion can represent two things: the pure sinless body of Christ and the extreme urgency for salvation as soon as possible. "Now is the day of salvation" (2 Cor. 6:2).

Time of Day

It's interesting that the Passover was celebrated at twilight. Although Jesus' death took place around 3:00 P.M., the Bible says that "darkness came over the land" (Matt. 27:45).

Blood of the Lamb

Then there was the blood of the Passover lamb that the Israelites were required to put on their doorposts and lintels. This actually painted in blood a type of cross over the entrance to their homes. Its purpose? To save the people of Israel when the Angel of Death passed over their homes, just as the blood of the Lamb over our hearts saves us from death (see Exod. 12:12,13; Matt. 26:27-29).

Finally, Jesus spoke of the cup of the Last Supper as representing His "new covenant" with believers (Luke 22:20). He told the disciples to continue to share the communion meal "in remembrance of" Him.

All this to say, what tremendous concepts and memories of Christ are renewed in our minds as we obey and celebrate this meal.

Day 2
Days of Remembrance

These are the Lord's appointed feasts, the sacred assemblies you are to proclaim at their appointed times. Leviticus 23:4

There was a time in my zeal for the Lord that I thought all holidays and celebrations were "indulgences of the flesh"—not something a serious Christian should be a part of. There were far too many things to do than sit around and pig out on Thanksgiving, buy out on Christmas, and collect-cavity causing candy eggs on Easter. After all I was a young warrior who had just given his life to Christ. There were just too many battles to fight for me to be seduced by such pagan rites.

Today I'm still not a big fan of Santa Claus and the Easter Bunny. There's something obscene about an overweight elf and a furry fertility symbol competing with the incarnation of God and His power over the grave. But I was really out-to-lunch to think the Lord frowned on celebrations and feast days. In fact it came as quite a shock for me to learn that He actually commanded the Jewish people to observe at least six different holidays—days when no work was to be done and when the Israelites simply had to rest and remember God's goodness.

How could this be? Didn't God know there's too much work to do to just sit around? Too many souls to save, too many hurt and broken people? How can we eat and play when others are starving, dying and quite literally going to hell?

It took several years for me to realize that my zeal had to be balanced. In my desire to work hard for the Lord, I was actually committing a sin—the sin of not giving God His full glory, the sin of thinking I'm too busy doing His work to enjoy Him and His goodness. To think my work was more important than resting and honoring my Father, was to make the same mistake that the Scribes and Pharisees made in Jesus' day. They were so busy serving that they forgot the One they were serving.

That's what the holidays and days of rest spoken of in the Old Testament are for: to "catch our breath" and to honor our Father. And, even though we are under the new covenant and no longer have to remember God's "legal holidays," they set a good principle for us to follow.

Let's find the time to rest and enjoy the holidays He's given us. They don't have to be times to pig out or put our homes up for ransom to MasterCard. But they should be times to appreciate, to rest, to remember and to glory in His goodness to us. That's what God would prefer.

In short, nothing should steal God's glory—not even our desire to serve Him.

Day 3
Remembrance Through Creation

Since the creation of the world God's invisible qualities—his eternal power and divine nature—have been clearly seen, being understood from what has been made, so that men are without excuse. Romans 1:20

As the Enemy keeps winding our lives up tighter and tighter, as we keep running faster and faster, I'm afraid one of the biggest areas in which we're being ripped off is in our enjoyment of Creation. I'm not talking about packing the kids off to a whirlwind tour of Grand Canyon. I mean simply taking the time to appreciate the day-to-day beauty and craftsmanship that surrounds us. If we're looking for symbols to remind us of Christ's love, creativity and care, what better place to look than to His handiwork.

And we don't have to live in the middle of Yellowstone either. That appreciation can happen anywhere. Take color for instance. Look around. Everything about us has or reflects some color. Take a moment. Enjoy it. Savor it. Marvel at the subtle differences and shades. It's interesting that the Lord didn't need to invent color. It serves no purpose. Our eyes could have been like dogs' eyes and only see black and white. But in His love and indulgence for us our Creator invented color.

Or how about sounds? An exercise I often take young actors through is to have them close their eyes and listen deeply for five minutes—listen past the roar of the highway, past the drone of an overhead plane, to the multitude of fragile and overlooked sounds that surround us every second.

What about trees? Have you ever seen such diversity? What an incredible variation on just one, single theme.

And, talk about variation, what about the Lord's crowning creation: human beings? Our faces, heights, personalities—the deep emotions running through each of us? Is there any limit to Christ's creativity and imagination?

One of my favorite books of all time is the Pulitzer Prize winner *Pilgrim at Tinker Creek*. In it the author, Annie Dillard, writes about the day-to-day activity around her creek. But not just the rompings of some playful chipmunk. She also marvels over a drop of swamp water under a microscope or a square inch of soil. The life, the diversity, the complexity and genius of creation in these tiny microcosms of the universe is astounding—wondrous—breathtaking.

Granted, rejoicing over a leaf ablaze with autumn color doesn't pay the mortgage or deal with the hundred and one migraine makers facing us each day. But enjoying creation from time to time can serve as a reminder of how in charge and detail orientated Christ really is. After all, there is no better way to truly know an artist's soul than to scrutinize his work. And there are few ways to better understand the depth of Jesus Christ than by marvelling over His masterpieces.

Day 4
Remembrance Through Parenthood

> *Which of you, if his son asks for bread, will give him a stone? Or if he asks for a fish, will give him a snake? If you, then, though you are evil, know how to give good gifts to your children, how much more will your Father in heaven give good gifts to those who ask him!* Matthew 7:9-11

For me there is no greater reminder of God's love than my love for my little daughter. Every day that she is with me my understanding of the Lord and His feelings towards me deepens.

The Lord's Love

My little daughter really changed my theology. I used to secretly think God was standing high upon a chair waiting to trounce on me whenever I messed up. Now I'm beginning to understand the pain and frustration the Lord feels when He sees me sinning. He's not fussing and fuming, waiting to clobber me. He's aching. He's as saddened when He sees me sin as when I see my daughter insist on doing the wrong thing and getting hurt by the consequences.

The Lord's Provision

I now understand that there's nothing Christ won't do for me. If it won't harm me or sacrifice the quality He's perfecting in my life or in others, He will do it for me. If my daughter needs something or even thinks she needs it, and I know it won't harm her by spoiling her character, I'll get it. I won't play hard to get, I won't taunt her, I won't make her jump through hoops. Instead, if it's her will and doesn't conflict with my will, she's got it.

The Lord's Sadness

At the moment my child is going through a phase where she doesn't want me around. She seems to be constantly nudging my hand aside and insisting on being by herself. Like the Lord, I respect that freewill choice. And, like the Lord, my heart is breaking.

The Lord's Anger

Three things outrage me:
1. My daughter blatantly disobeying me and insisting upon hurting herself by carrying out her own stubborn will;

2. Someone else hurting her;

3. When her efforts to do the right thing are frustrated.

In each and every one of those situations I will immediately be at her side doing everything in my power to discipline, to intercede or to help.

The Lord's Forgiveness

One thing melts me faster than anything else—when my daughter comes into the room, head bowed, sometimes even in tears and sincerely says, "Daddy, I'm sorry. Would you forgive me?"

How could I do otherwise?

All this to say, sometimes we don't have to look any further than our own families to see and remember our Lord.

Day 5
Remembrance Through the Sabbath

Remember the Sabbath day by keeping it holy.
Six days you shall labor and do all your work,
but the seventh day is a Sabbath to the Lord
your God. On it you shall not do any work,
neither you, nor your son or daughter, nor your
manservant or maidservant, nor your animals,
nor the alien within your gates. For in six days
the Lord made the heavens and the earth, the
sea, and all that is in them, but he rested on the
seventh day. Therefore the Lord blessed the
Sabbath day and made it holy. Exodus 20:8-11

My brother and I were having an interesting discussion on theology when he asked me this question: "If you look upon the Ten Commandments as good principles to guide your walk as a Christian, why do you only follow nine out of those ten principles? Why aren't you as committed to the principle of setting aside one day a week to honor the Lord as you are to the principles of not stealing or not coveting?"

He had me. We weren't arguing about a specific day, just any day—any total day that I would stop what I was doing and rest, honor and remember the Lord.

My brother does keep this principle as well as the nine others. And during my visits to his home I always enjoy that entire day being set aside for remembering the Lord and for the peace, fellowship and simple pleasure of friends and family. There are no blaring TVs, video games or frantic trips to the mall—just a quiet appreciation of others and of Jesus Christ.

My wife and I eventually followed suit. Now we don't set aside the same day as my brother. As a Seventh Day Adventist he worships on Saturday instead of Sunday. But we do understand the need to set aside a special time for resting and remembering God's love and faithfulness.

Perhaps in contemporary Christian zeal to be free of the Law and all of its trappings and traditions, many Christians have somehow short-changed themselves and missed out on a major principle of life: the need for rest. God emphasized this need when after creating the world "on the seventh day he rested from all His work" (Gen. 2:2).

I believe that it pleases the Lord when we set aside one day a week to cease from our labors, our worldly pursuits, even some of our worldly pleasures and to focus upon Him. I believe that there is a seven day cycle that He has created and that after six days of labor, especially in today's hectic, fast track world, we need to clear our minds of that world. We need to set aside that day for our refreshment, our rest and His glory.

I don't believe this means a quick morning in church followed by hectic shopping sprees, a raunchy double feature at the cineplex and a race home to catch "60 Minutes."

My family doesn't follow any specific rules or regulations. But by adhering to the basic principle of honoring and resting one day a week, our lives seem fuller and more relaxed. And above all, for at least one day a week we are able to dwell with Jesus more thoroughly and remember Him more clearly.

Day 6
Our Heritage

We have heard with our ears, O God; our fathers have told us what you did in their days, in days long ago. Psalm 44:1

On a recent film project in Red China I was sharing a hotel room with my translator, a British brother closely associated with the Anglican Church. It was early morning and as we prepared for the day we were both humming and singing quiet songs of worship to ourselves. But when my friend got into the shower he suddenly cut loose. I mean the walls were practically vibrating. And his song was gorgeous. It was full of such rich melody, texture and meaning that it made my little sing-songy praise chorus sound like a nursery rhyme.

I stopped. Not because I had to, but because listening to his song was more of a blessing than me singing mine. In fact, that's how I spent my quiet time before the Lord that morning—just listening to my friend singing in the shower!

Later I learned that the hymn was nearly a century old. And yet, it seemed far more relevant than my hip, upbeat, little ditty.

How many other things have I deprived myself of in the name of what is "modern and happening"?

As Christians we have a tremendous culture and heritage that stretches back hundreds upon hundreds of years. Traditions, old hymns, ancient and magnificently sung masses that glorify Christ, as well as writings by ancient Church fathers that carry more depth and meaning in one paragraph than a dozen of our contemporary books.

I'm not suggesting that we embrace every creed and thought from the past. What I am suggesting is this:

As we look for new ways to keep our faith alive and vibrant, as we use fresh and innovative ways of worshiping and remembering God, let's not be so egocentric as to think that our generation has all the answers. Let's not throw out nineteen centuries of heritage.

We have a rich and beautiful history of brothers and sisters dedicated to Christ. Their works can provide plenty of relevant light to rekindle even the dimmest flames of faith.

A great scientist when praised for his discoveries said, "I only stand on the shoulders of past giants." We too have giant shoulders we can stand upon in our efforts to draw closer to the heart of God.

8
RECONCILED!

Therefore, brothers, since we have confidence to enter the Most Holy Place by the blood of Jesus, by a new and living way opened for us through the curtain, that is, his body...let us draw near to God with a sincere heart in full assurance of faith. Hebrews 10:19,20,22

We've spent some time covering Christ's work on the cross—how on that day He redeemed us, how His blood made us righteous, how He served as the Lamb of God, and how He became our great, High Priest.

To underscore the significance of His crucifixion, the Lord caused several interesting phenomena to occur. The first and most graphic was the tearing of the Temple curtain.

The curtain was probably 30 to 40 feet in height and as thick as the palm of the hand. Its purpose was to separate the people in the Temple from the presence of God who dwelt in the Most Holy Place or innermost compartment of the Temple. Only the High Priest was allowed behind the curtain and only once a year after he had been ceremonially cleansed of his sins.

But at the exact moment of Christ's payment on the cross, the Temple curtain was completely torn in two—from top to bottom—from heaven to earth (see Matt. 27:51).

This tearing was no coincidence. (Consider the height and the thickness of the curtain.) And it was no minor miracle. Its meaning could not have been more clear. Suddenly everybody had complete and total access to the presence of God!

But this was not the only phenomena that took place in the Temple. The Jewish historian, Josephus, also talks about the center and main light in the golden candlestick mysteriously going out.

Then there were the huge Temple gates. Both Josephus and the Jewish Talmud mention that the gates, which had previously been closed, strangely and supernaturally opened up on their own.

The Bible also talks about a darkness that "came over the whole land" for three hours during Jesus' final suffering (Mark 15:33). An eclipse? Possibly. A symbol of mankind's attempt to extinguish God's great Light? Definitely.

Then there was the tremendous earthquake. We're not talking small time tremor here. The quake was so intense that it actually split rocks open. But it was not only rocks that were opened...

> *The tombs broke open and the bodies of many*
> *holy people who had died were raised to life.*
> *They came out of the tombs, and after Jesus'*
> *resurrection they went into the holy city and*
> *appeared to many people.*
> Matthew 27:52,53

It seems that our Lord was definitely making a point with all of these supernatural events. He was making it clear that this was not just another crucifixion. This was God in human form, buying back the souls of humanity through

His sacrifice on the cross. The supernatural occurrences were merely seals underscoring the validity of that agreement—of that reconciliation.

Day 2
The Need for Reconciliation

God is a righteous judge, a God who expresses his wrath every day. Psalm 7:11

Today when everybody seems to be oversimplifying God by summing Him up as, "Love," it's hard to see any real need for reconciliation with Him.

As a result the cross becomes simply a symbol of that love and not a real necessity. *After all,* they figure, *"God is love." He'll accept me. What do I have to worry about?*

But without Jesus the answer is "PLENTY." To help us get a fuller picture of our Father and the need for reconciliation with Him, it might be a good idea to take a look at His feelings about disobedience:

> *You shall not make for yourself an idol....for I, the Lord your God, am a jealous God, punishing the children for the sin of the fathers to the third and fourth generation of those who hate me.* Exodus 20:4,5

> *Do not take advantage of a widow or an orphan. If you do and they cry out to me, I will certainly hear their cry. My anger will be aroused, and I will kill you with the sword; your wives will become widows and your children fatherless.* Exodus 22:22-24

> *They came as a group to oppose Moses and Aaron....The Lord said to Moses and Aaron, "Separate yourselves from this assembly so I can put an end to them at once."*
> Numbers 16:3,20,21

> *The Lord's anger burned against Israel and he made them wander in the desert forty years, until the whole generation of those who had done evil in his sight was gone.* Numbers 32:13

> *Do not follow other gods, the gods of the peoples around you; for the Lord your God, who is among you, is a jealous God and his anger will burn against you, and he will destroy you from the face of the land.* Deuteronomy 6:14,15

And for those who think that God somehow changed His outlook on disobedience by the time the New Testament rolled around:

> *The wrath of God is being revealed from heaven against all the godlessness and wickedness of men who suppress the truth by their wickedness.*
> Romans 1:18

> *The king* [a symbol of God in this parable] *was enraged. He sent his army and destroyed those murderers and burned their city.* Matthew 22:7

> *Let no one deceive you with empty words, for because of such things God's wrath comes on those who are disobedient.* Ephesians 5:6

And God's reaction to sin in the future? Well, since He's unchanging, things will be no different:

Then the kings of the earth, the princes, the generals, the rich, the mighty, and every slave and every free man hid in caves and among the rocks of the mountains. They called to the mountains and the rocks, "Fall on us and hide us from the face of him who sits on the throne and from the wrath of the Lamb! For the great day of their wrath has come, and who can stand?" Revelation 6:15-17

When the world thinks of God they seldom think of someone who burns with anger, who is intensely jealous, whose wrath brings judgment. As a result they may not see a need for reconciliation with Him. But regardless of the world's view of God, when it comes to rebellion and sin, this anger, jealousy and wrath are exactly what our Lord feels.

Fortunately, we never need to experience this wrath—if we accept His solution—if we accept His Son.

Day 3
The Great Reconciler

Then I saw in the right hand of him who sat on the throne a scroll with writing on both sides and sealed with seven seals. And I saw a mighty angel proclaiming in a loud voice, "Who is worthy to break the seals and open the scroll?" But no one in heaven or on earth or under the earth could open the scroll or even look inside it. I wept and wept because no one was found who was worthy to open the scroll or look inside. Then one of the elders said to me, "Do not weep! See, the Lion of the tribe of Judah, the Root of David, has triumphed. He is able to open the scroll and its seven seals."

> *Then I saw a Lamb, looking as if it had been slain, standing in the center of the throne, encircled by the four living creatures and the elders. He had seven horns and seven eyes, which are the seven spirits of God sent out into all the earth. He came and took the scroll from the right hand of him who sat on the throne. And when he had taken it, the four living creatures and the twenty-four elders fell down before the Lamb. Each one had a harp and they were holding golden bowls full of incense, which are the prayers of the saints. And they sang a new song:*
>
> *"You are worthy to take the scroll and to open its seals, because you were slain, and with your blood you purchased men for God from every tribe and language and people and nation. You have made them to be a kingdom and priests to serve our God, and they will reign on the earth.* Revelation 5:1-10

This is one of my all time favorite passages of Scripture. Picture it. God the Father is holding the title deed to the earth, the deed to our very souls, the deed that was given away to Satan so many years before in the Garden of Eden. He is holding it in His hand and asks if anybody is worthy to take it. But no one, absolutely no one in the entire universe, steps forward. John, the one given this vision of the future, breaks into tremendous weeping over our hopelessness, the hopelessness of the human race. There is no one worthy to take that deed, no one who can redeem us.

Then suddenly, in His various symbolic forms, including the "Lamb, who was slain," (Rev. 5:12), Jesus Christ appears. He boldly strides forward and takes the title deed into His hand.

What a glorious, triumphant scene that must have been.

Only Jesus Christ is able to step forward. Only Jesus Christ is able to redeem us. Only Jesus Christ is worthy to take the deed to our world, to buy us back, to reconcile us!

Day 4
Jubilation!

If one of your countrymen becomes poor among you and sells himself to you, do not make him work as a slave. He is to be treated as a hired worker or a temporary resident among you; he is to work for you until the Year of Jubilee. Then he and his children are to be released, and he will go back to his own clan and to the property of his forefathers. Leviticus 25:39-41

There is another foreshadowing of Christ's reconciliation in the Old Testament. It was called the "Year of Jubilee."

The Lord commanded the Jewish people that every fiftieth year all of their debts to one another were to be totally and completely canceled (see Lev. 25). Picture it, any debts or bills that anyone had run up through their own negligence or even corruptness were completely wiped clean!

It would be as if the charges on your Visa Card suddenly came up $00. As if the mortgage on your house was miraculously paid in full. And while we're at it, kiss those car and school payments good-bye. Talk about release—talk about being free to start fresh! But there's more...

All lands that had been sold were to be returned to the original owner. Why? Because the Lord said, "The land is mine and you are but aliens and my tenants" (Lev. 25:23). So if you had gotten into a financial fix and had to sell your land, during the Year of Jubilee it would be returned to you so you could start anew.

And finally, all of the slaves were to be set free. What a beautiful symbol of our future release from the slavery of sin through Jesus Christ!

The concept of the Year of Jubilee was revolutionary. It was a picture of reconciliation. Talk about "setting the captives free." During the Year of Jubilee no one was enslaved or bound by anything or anybody. There are few if any practices that more clearly demonstrate God's understanding of our tendency to get into bondage and His mercy towards setting us free.

It was this freedom that Jesus may have had in mind when He officially announced His ministry in His local synagogue:

> *He has sent me to proclaim freedom for the prisoners and recovery of sight for the blind, to release the oppressed, to proclaim the year of the Lord's favor.* Luke 4:18,19

Jesus Christ is our Year of Jubilee. But fortunately we don't have to wait fifty years. Because His payment was so complete our Jubilee can take place as often as we say a prayer!

Day 5
Our Responsibility

> *If we claim to be without sin, we deceive ourselves and the truth is not in us. If we confess our sins, he is faithful and just and will forgive us our sins and purify us from all unrighteousness.* 1 John 1:8,9

Not more than half an hour ago I experienced such a liberating experience that I have to write it down now while it's still fresh in my memory.

Several months ago I went through an excruciating time

in a business situation. I was caught in the middle of some pretty ambitious forces and, as a result, I got mauled and beat up quite badly. It was unjust, unfair and probably the most painful time of my professional career.

I know bitterness and anger are wrong. I know they can eat into you emotionally making you a double victim. And I know they can eat into you physically (which explains the burning ache in my stomach). But I just couldn't seem to get rid of the anger. Even though I asked the Lord to remove it, it just kept on coming back.

Once again, this morning I was trying to spend some time in prayer and, sure enough, the situation rose in my mind as it has a dozen times a day for the past several months. Once again I found myself chewing and mulling over the injustice of it all. I kept trying to push it out of my mind so I could pray, but it kept returning until finally the time I had set aside for prayer was over.

Soon a brother appeared at my door and wanted to pray over a financial problem in his life. But as we were praying for him, it suddenly came to my mind that I wasn't just angry with those involved in my business deal—I actually hated them. That's right—hated. What a shock. Me, Mr. Mature Christian, actually hated someone.

But Christians don't hate, I thought.

Maybe they're not supposed to, but I sure did. As the prayer over my friend's finances was closing, I couldn't stand it any longer. I blurted out a confession of my hate. I finally admitted the truth and asked God to forgive me. No religious piety. No soft pedaling. Just honesty: "I hate and I can't help myself." No sooner had the words come out of my mouth then the cloud surrounding my head these many months started to clear.

What liberation! What freedom!

It was so simple, but so against my human nature (especially since I thought of myself as too mature to be dealing with such basics).

From the time of the Garden of Eden until now, we humans have tried to gloss over our sins, to sanitize them, or worse yet, pass the buck. "It wasn't me," Adam insisted. "It was that woman you gave me." And Eve's great defense? "It wasn't me. It was the serpent."

If we could just keep in mind that we only have one responsibility in reconciliation: We must honestly, and I stress the word *honestly*, confess our sins before our Father. If we do, not only will He forgive us, but He will also clean and purify us!

Does this mean that I'll magically stop hating those who've hurt me? Probably not. But I can tell you I'm a lot closer to it now than I was an hour ago. And, as I continue to be honest and faithful in confessing my sin, He will be faithful to forgive me and purify me "from all unrighteousness."

Day 6
Forgiveness and Forgetfulness

I, even I, am he who blots out your
transgressions, for my own sake, and
remembers your sins no more. Isaiah 43:25

A good friend of mine once made a terrific point. "Do you know," he asked, "that there's something we can do that God can't?"

"What's that?" I asked, rising to the challenge.

"We can remember our past sins."

He definitely caught me off guard. It was true, but I had never really stopped to consider the depth of that truth. Basically, like everyone else I figured the old adage, "I may forgive, but I won't forget," also applied to God.

But nothing could be more wrong. God does not sit on His throne and grudgingly forgive us with the attitude of

"Well, I'll let it go this time, but just you wait." No. The price Jesus paid for our reconciliation with the Father was so expensive, so complete, that God not only forgives our sins but He actually forgets them!

What freedom! What joy to know that the Father's loving arms are always open to us with no strings or past grudges attached.

Keep that in mind the next time the "accuser of our brothers" brings up your past in an attempt to paralyze you with guilt (Rev. 12:10). Satan can't get anywhere by bringing your past sins up to the Father because the Father refuses to remember. So the only person the Devil can torment with your past is you.

Don't fall for it. If God in all of His glory refuses to remember or listen to your past, who are you to think you should?

When we commit our lives to Christ, you and I are free and completely reconciled to the Father. Nothing can ever come between us again—not even our past failures, no matter how despicable, no matter how recurring, no matter how recent. Because of Christ's blood the Father now and always will see us as perfect and love us as deeply and as purely as He loves His only begotten Son.

9
GOD'S RICH
STREAM OF MERCY

*Make an atonement cover of pure gold....And
make two cherubim out of hammered gold at
the ends of the cover....The cherubim are to face
each other, looking toward the cover. Place the
cover on top of the ark and put in the ark the
Testimony, which I will give you. There, above
the cover between the two cherubim that are
over the ark of the Testimony, I will meet with
you and give you all my commands for the
Israelites.* Exodus 25:17,18,20-22.

The focus of the Tabernacle and later the Temple was
the Ark of the Covenant. It was the Ark that was separated
from the people by the curtain. It was the Ark that was kept
inside the Holy of Holies. And it was directly above the Ark
that God's very presence, His Shekinah Glory, dwelt. With
this in mind, it shouldn't come as much of a surprise that
the Ark and its contents also served as strong symbols of
who God is.

For starters, the Ark was about the size of a small hope
chest—2 1/4 feet high x 2 1/4 feet wide and 3 3/4 feet long.

It was made of acacia wood: a hard, heavy, close-grain wood impenetrable by insects—a symbol of God's indestructible nature. The Ark was overlaid with pure gold, symbolizing God's purity and holiness.

Inside were the tablets of the Ten Commandments (symbolizing God's demand for our holiness), a pot of manna collected in the wilderness (symbolizing God's care and provision) and Aaron's staff which God had at one point turned into a snake and at another caused to bud, bloom and produce almonds overnight (symbolizing God's power; see Exod. 7:10; Num. 17:8).

The lid was made of solid gold with a cherub (a type of angel) at each end. They faced the center with their wings spread out over it. God referred to this lid as the "atonement cover" or "mercy seat." On this cover was sprinkled the sacrificial blood of animals to atone for sin. Over this cover God's actual presence dwelt.

It was here, at the exact center of God's presence, that the two greatest aspects of God's character are united—His holiness, represented by the pure gold of the mercy seat and His mercy, represented by the actual mercy seat itself.

It's interesting to note that it was not called the judgment seat, the holy seat, the power seat or any of the other attributes of God. God chose to call the very seat that He dwelt upon "the mercy seat." And that should tell us something about the emphasis He puts upon mercy.

Day 2
Mercy and Justice

The teachers of the law and the Pharisees brought in a woman caught in adultery. They made her stand before the group and said to Jesus, "Teacher, this woman was caught in the act of adultery. In the Law Moses commanded

*us to stone such women. Now what do you
say?" They were using this question as a trap, in
order to have a basis for accusing him.*

*But Jesus bent down and started to write on
the ground with his finger. When they kept on
questioning him, he straightened up and said to
them, "If any one of you is without sin, let him
be the first to throw a stone at her."...*

*At this, those who heard began to go away
one at a time, the older ones first, until only
Jesus was left, with the woman still standing
there. Jesus straightened up and asked her,
"Woman, where are they? Has no one
condemned you?"*

"No one, sir," she said.

*"Then neither do I condemn you," Jesus
declared. "Go now and leave your life of sin."*
John 8:3-11

Like this woman I am guilty of adultery. I may not be
having a sexual affair but I am definitely guilty of carrying
on relationships with other gods: gods of mammon, gods of
self, gods of materialism and gods of pride. In short, I've
been having quite a hot and steamy love affair with the gods
of this world.

Like the woman I am caught, red-handed—forced to
stand before my Lord with absolutely no defense. There is
nothing I can say. I am guilty. I know it. He knows it. And
according to the law I must die (see Deut. 6:14,15; also 1
Cor. 6:9). All that is right and fair and just insists that I must
die.

But instead of sentencing me to death, my Lord looks
up to me and simply says, "I do not condemn you. Go and
sin no more."

How can this be? How can I suddenly be free, totally
innocent? How can God maintain His perfect standard of

justice and holiness and yet completely let me off the hook?

This was the same question the Pharisees struggled with as they tried to trap Jesus. Which is truth: God's justice of the Old Testament or Christ's "new" concept of mercy?

And Jesus' answer? Both.

Jesus never said the woman was not guilty. He never said she should not be killed. Instead, He pointed out that only someone totally holy and free from sin should carry out that death sentence. And, once that was clearly understood, Jesus became the judge and executioner. But the execution wasn't carried out at that time, nor was it upon this woman. Instead, our holy and sinless God carried out the sentence just a little bit later. He carried it out upon Himself.

Day 3
The Breadth of Mercy

> *The Lord is compassionate and gracious, slow to anger, abounding in love. He will not always accuse, nor will he harbor his anger forever; he does not treat us as our sins deserve or repay us according to our iniquities. For as high as the heavens are above the earth, so great is his love for those who fear him; as far as the east is from the west, so far has he removed our transgressions from us. As a father has compassion on his children, so the Lord has compassion on those who fear him.*
> Psalm 103:8-13

How extensive is Christ's mercy? Can we exhaust it? Can we somehow use it up? In short: Can you and I lose our salvation? This is a difficult question and as I pointed out before, I'm not a theologian, but I would like to share with you some thoughts.

The very fact that Jesus chose to leave His high position in heaven and come down to suffer and give up His life for a civilization that hated and despised Him, is a pretty good indication of the breadth of His love.

Also, praying for the people that drove the nails through His hands and feet, crying out to the Father to forgive those who were torturing Him is another clear indication of the magnitude of His mercy.

And finally there is the excruciating agony of taking all of our sins upon Himself, of enduring all of the Father's wrath for our disobedience.

When you stop and think about it, these make up a pretty hefty down payment that Jesus Christ paid for our souls. We've cost Him dearly. So it's doubtful He's going to let any of us slip out of His hands.

And yet, there are Bible passages that indicate that not everyone who thinks he is saved, is saved. Or as Jesus put it:

> Not everyone who says to me, "Lord, Lord,"
> will enter the kingdom of heaven, but only he
> who does the will of my Father who is in
> heaven. Matthew 7:21

So what gives? Is there a limit to Christ's mercy? Can we exhaust it?

As a youth worker I'm frequently met with this question. It usually comes from two types of kids: those who are sincerely trying to do what the Lord wants and are afraid that if they fail they're going to hell, and those who want to know how far they can go and still slip into heaven. To the kids who are serious but fail I say, "No, there is absolutely no limit to Christ's mercy for you." To the kids who are looking for loopholes and ways to walk as close to the edge as possible I say, "Yes, there is definitely a possibility of losing your salvation."

Am I lying? No. I sincerely believe both answers are true. I believe it is the attitude of the heart that God looks at and not some computer scoreboard of our victories and defeats. I believe that if we are sincerely trying to follow Christ He will sincerely forgive us. But if we are only using Him and playing a game, we may be surprised by who comes out the loser.

Perhaps a good friend of mine puts it best. Whenever he's asked if there's a limit to Christ's mercy, if we can lose our salvation, he simply says, "No, we cannot lose our salvation. But if we work hard enough at it, we can certainly throw it away."

Day 4
The Depth of Christ's Mercy

Consider it pure joy, my brothers, whenever you face trials of many kinds, because you know that the testing of your faith develops perseverance. Perseverance must finish its work so that you may be mature and complete, not lacking anything. James 1:2-4

Just as I believe that for the sincere there is no end to the breadth of God's mercy, I also believe that there is no end to the depth of His mercy. I believe that the Lord's mercy can be so deep, so profound, that often, at first glance, it appears to be anything but mercy. Often, at first glance, it may even appear to be the opposite of mercy.

C.S. Lewis probably put this best in a letter to a friend who had just lost his wife. He explained that his friend was undergoing the Lord's "severe mercy."

Although there are many cases in Scripture and history that illustrate this severe mercy, the story of young Billy Graham is one of the most poignant. This is not only because of the obvious fruit his life and ministry have born, but also because there are few things as painful to a young man as a broken heart.

It seems young Graham had fallen head over heels in love with a college sweetheart. She was his joy, his love, the woman he wanted to spend his life with. But when he finally got around to popping the question, her answer was no.

"But why?" he persisted, not believing his ears.

"Because you're not spiritual enough," she replied.

Graham was crushed. Devastated. But deep inside he knew she was right. He knew there was still too much of the world in his life. As a result, he began to seriously evaluate his spirituality. And he eventually began to seek and commit himself more deeply to Jesus Christ.

The pain in young Graham's heart must have been immeasurable. But now, as he looks back, Reverend Graham sees that pain as absolutely necessary in refocusing and shaping his life into the ministry it is today. And I'm sure that today Billy Graham looks upon that past heartache as an example of the depth of Christ's mercy.

The Lord's mercy may not always come as beautifully wrapped gifts. It may come disguised as heartache, unbearable pain and excruciating pressures. But Christ has not deserted us. His mercy continues in our lives on every level—even the deepest, most severe level.

Yet, if we allow Him, if we fully trust Him, He will take the intense pain and pressure surrounding us and use it to transform the rough, black coal of our hearts into the precious, eternal diamonds of His image.

Day 5
Deeper Depth

> *The Lord heard you when you wailed, "If only*
> *we had meat to eat! We were better off in*
> *Egypt!" Now the Lord will give you meat, and*
> *you will eat it. You will not eat it for just one*
> *day, or two days, or five, ten or twenty days, but*
> *for a whole month—until it comes out of your*
> *nostrils and you loathe it—because you have*
> *rejected the Lord, who is among you, and have*
> *wailed before him, saying, "Why did we ever*
> *leave Egypt?"* Numbers 11:18-20

There is another aspect to the depth of the Lord's mercy that we seldom examine. Sometimes, if we want something so badly, if we will not rest until we get it, if we resent the Lord for withholding it, if our attitude becomes rebellious for not receiving it, Christ, in the depth of His mercy, will eventually let us have it. This was the case with the children of Israel on at least two separate occasions.

In the wilderness the Israelites were sick and tired of eating manna, the food the Lord so graciously and miraculously supplied for them on a daily basis. But this supernatural provision wasn't good enough for them. They wanted meat, meat like other people ate, meat like they had back in the "good old days"—you know, when they were slaves in Egypt.

The people continued to gripe and complain and bellyache until the Lord finally had enough. He let them have their way.

They wanted meat? They got meat. A gigantic flock of quail flew over and crashed into the camp. There were so many that they covered the ground as far as a man could walk in a day! Now at last the people had meat. But, as a result, Scripture says God allowed a plague to fall upon them and, "while the meat was still between their teeth," the people who craved meat died (Num. 11:33).

Then there was the situation in 1 Samuel 8. The people wanted a king like everyone else. But the Lord had in essence told them, "You're not like everyone else. I've got something better for you."

God had Samuel warn the people about the excesses of kings (see 1 Sam. 8:10-18). Yet they kept asking, and whining and complaining until He finally gave in and let them have their way. A way which proved far inferior to the blessings He originally had in mind for them.

The depth of the Lord's mercy is unfathomable. He will go to any extent, even letting us have our own, stubborn, self-willed way if it will eventually draw us closer to His blessings and His ways.

Often our first choice is His last choice. Sometimes our choices will cause us pain. But if it's the only way we can learn, God will grant us our desires. If it is the only way we can learn to trust Him and fully enter the "abundant life" He promised, then our Lord will spare no expense to help us enter that life, even if it means letting us fall into the awful and terrible hands of our own self will.

Day 6
Mercy Towards Others

Forgive us our debts, as we also have forgiven our debtors. Matthew 6:12

For any of us who have prayed the Lord's Prayer but have not forgiven or shown mercy towards another, well, we could be in a bit of trouble. By praying this portion of the Lord's Prayer we are actually asking for the Father to forgive us on the basis of how we forgive others: "Forgive us *as we forgive.*" And if we haven't forgiven others, well, let's just say things could get sticky on judgment day.

To make sure we understand the importance of this principle, the importance of passing on the mercy the Lord so freely gave us, the Bible records a fascinating discussion Jesus had with Peter. It seems Peter thought that forgiving someone seven times was gracious enough. Jesus disagreed and made it clear that seventy-seven times was closer to what He had in mind. Then to further underline His point, Jesus went on to deliver the following parable:

> *The kingdom of heaven is like a king who wanted to settle accounts with his servants. As he began the settlement, a man who owed him ten thousand talents* [millions of dollars] *was brought to him. Since he was not able to pay, the master ordered that he and his wife and his children and all that he had be sold to repay the debt.*
>
> *The servant fell on his knees before him. "Be patient with me," he begged, "and I will pay back everything." The servant's master took pity on him, canceled the debt and let him go.*
>
> *But when the servant went out, he found one of his fellow servants who owed him a hundred denarii* [a few dollars]. *He grabbed him and began to choke him. "Pay back what you owe me!" he demanded.*
>
> *His fellow servant fell to his knees and begged him, "Be patient with me, and I will pay you back."*
>
> *But he refused. Instead, he went off and had the man thrown into prison until he*

*could pay the debt. When the other servants
saw what had happened, they were greatly
distressed and went and told their master
everything that had happened.*

*Then the master called the servant in.
"You wicked servant," he said, "I canceled
all that debt of yours because you begged me
to. Shouldn't you have had mercy on your
fellow servant just as I had on you?" In
anger his master turned him over to the
jailers to be tortured, until he should pay
back all he owed.*

*This is how my heavenly Father will treat
each of you unless you forgive your brother
from your heart.* Matthew 18:23-35

He has forgiven us so much, how can we not forgive
others?

Grace is a rich stream that flows from the throne of
heaven. Not only should we let it flow into our hearts, but
we should let it pass through us in the form of forgiveness
of others.

10
AMAZING GRACE

*Just as Moses lifted up the snake in the desert,
so the Son of Man must be lifted up, that
everyone who believes in him may have eternal
life.* John 3:14,15

In John 3 we read about Jesus trying to explain to
Nicodemus (a godly Pharisee) the basic principles of the
Lord's grace. Jesus really had His work cut out for Him!
Nicodemus, like many of us, was so busy trying to be
religious, so busy trying to earn God's grace and pleasure,
that he completely missed the main point.

At first Jesus tried explaining that Nicodemus' only
responsibility was to believe and be born again (v.3). But,
true to form, the old timer immediately turned it into
something he had to work towards: "How can a man be
born when he is old?...Surely he cannot enter a second time
into his mother's womb to be born!" (v.4).

So Jesus tried another tack. He reminded Nicodemus of
the time the children of Israel were wandering in the desert
and began actively complaining and rebelling against God. As
judgment, the Lord sent "venomous snakes" into the camp

that bit the people and caused many to die (see Num. 21:4-9).

Realizing their sin, the people repented. To save them from dying, God told Moses to make a bronze snake and put it high upon a pole and all who looked upon it could be healed.

The people were helpless. They could do nothing to save themselves. No religious ceremonies, no religious works. All they could do was look towards the creature on the pole. The rest was up to God. It was His work, His grace. God did the healing. God did the saving.

This was the point Jesus was making to Nicodemus. The man's religious works added nothing to his salvation. It was all God's grace.

And the same is true for us. We can't earn salvation. We can't even earn His love. We don't have to work, we don't have to strive, we don't have to weary ourselves by being religious. All we have to do is repent and look to Him who was put high upon a "pole" for all to see. All we have to do is believe in Him who was lifted up and God's grace will do the rest.

Our job is to only need and ask. God's job is to save.

Day 2
No Expiration Date

You see, at just the right time, when we were still powerless, Christ died for the ungodly. Very rarely will anyone die for a righteous man, though for a good man someone might possibly dare to die. But God demonstrates his own love for us in this: While we were still sinners, Christ died for us. Since we have now been justified by his blood, how much more shall we be saved from God's wrath through him! For if, when we were God's enemies, we were reconciled to him through the death of his Son, how much more, having been reconciled, shall we be saved through his life! Romans 5:6-10

There are areas in my life that I am struggling with. Areas that I can't seem to let go of. Or maybe I can let go of them but simply don't want to. Maybe it's rebellion, maybe it's weakness, maybe it's just plain laziness that causes me to give in to the battles without a proper fight. I don't know. All I know is that I'm discouraged and frequently feel like something at the very bottom of the food chain. All I know is that if being with Christ and shedding this putrefying flesh and its sins is all there is to heaven, well, that's good enough for me.

But I know one other thing. I know that...

> *there is now no condemnation for those who are in Christ Jesus.* Romans 8:1

I know that no matter how many times I fail, no matter how many times I sin—I'm still forgiven.

"But how do you know?" the accuser demands. "You wretched hypocrite—preaching righteousness to others but failing in your own life. Maybe God forgave you when you were a baby Christian and didn't know any better, but not now. Now, you should be further along, now you should be more mature. Who're you kidding? There's no forgiveness for you. Not anymore!"

Wrong. Absolutely wrong. Not only is Christ's grace strong enough to break sin's controlling power over me—it is also strong enough to forgive me when I fail to trust that strength.

His grace never fails. I cannot use it up. It makes no difference how long I've lived and walked with Christ. It makes no difference how much I know or how much I have experienced. There is no age or maturity limit to His grace.

That's the point Paul is making in this section of Romans. If Christ loved and forgave me when I was His enemy and wanted to sin, how much more will He love and forgive me now that I love Him and don't want to sin?

Is this a license for older saints to disobey? Absolutely

not. It is however, an encouragement for us to stop listening to the accuser's voice when he tries to make us feel lost. It is a reminder that Jesus is still on our side when we fail—just as He was when we were first saved.

> *If we confess our sins, he is faithful and just and will forgive us our sins and purify us from all unrighteousness.* 1 John 1:9

This verse is just as true in our lives today a it was when we first heard it.

Day 3
The Greatness of Grace

> *He [Jesus Christ] is the image of the invisible God, the firstborn over all creation. For by him all things were created: things in heaven and on earth, visible and invisible, whether thrones or powers or rulers or authorities; all things were created by him and for him. He is before all things, and in him all things hold together.* Colossians 1:15-17

Picture it: The Creator of all things personally came to earth. He left all of His glory in heaven to live in the decaying body of a sin-racked race amidst a sin-ravaged world. (The closest thing we can compare this to is if we chose to leave the human family and joined a population of maggots somewhere.)

Then He put up with all of humanity's egotistical pride, verbal abuses and hatred—a hatred so intense that it caused people to plot His torture and crucifixion.

But (and this is where it really gets interesting) when He was on the cross He still didn't call it quits. Although Jesus could command a battalion of angels to swoop down and destroy His tormentors in a second, He didn't. People were standing at the foot of His cross, hurdling insults, mocking, taunting, defiling every trace of His holiness. Yet He still refused to destroy them. Instead He chose to lay down His life for them (see John 10:17,18). Talk about self-restraint. Talk about grace.

But there's more. Not only did He refuse to destroy them, not only did He lay down His life for them, but He was actually busy keeping them alive! That's right. According to Colossians 1:15-17, as Jesus Christ was being crucified, some how, some way, He was supernaturally holding together the very people who were torturing Him!

And in him all things hold together. Colossians 1:17

Talk about love! Talk about grace!

I mean it's one thing to resist hurdling your wrath down from heaven to wipe out the indignant loud mouths—but quite another to be actively keeping those loud mouths alive! Yet, that's exactly what Christ did.

This is the greatness of Christ's grace. The next time we begin to doubt His love or power to forgive, let's bring to memory the unlimited grace He displayed on the cross—not only forgiving the people that were torturing Him to death, but actually keeping them alive.

With that in mind, we can rest assured that we're not going to exhaust Christ's grace with whatever weaknesses we're currently struggling to overcome.

Day 4
Grace Versus Works

For it is by grace you have been saved, through faith—and this not from yourselves, it is the gift of God—not by works, so that no one can boast. Ephesians 2:8,9

Most of us have heard or recited these verses for years. But we've also heard this section from James:

> *What good is it, my brothers, if a man claims to have faith but has no deeds? Can such faith save him?....Show me your faith without deeds, and I will show you my faith by what I do. You believe that there is one God. Good! Even the demons believe that—and shudder....As the body without the spirit is dead, so faith without deeds is dead.*
> James 2:14,18,19,26

So what gives? Which saves us, faith or deeds? This is no light question. In fact the supposed contradiction haunted Martin Luther so badly that he wanted to throw the entire book of James out of the Bible!

But there really is no contradiction. Like so many aspects of the Christian walk, the answer is not "either/or." It is "both." The Christian walk is a series of balances, not extremes.

Yes, we are saved only by God's grace. But if our salvation does not bring about works, if it does not bear fruit, then it is dead. If I plant a fruit tree and it does not bear leaves, buds and fruit, then I no longer have a fruit tree—I have firewood.

Does that mean that once I'm saved I have to dig in and start working to keep my salvation?

No. The works will come as naturally to your living faith as fruit comes to a living tree. You don't have to strain, you don't have to sweat. All you have to do is abide and stay connected to Christ. The grace of God will do the rest, as effortlessly as a fruit tree bears fruit.

> *By their fruit you will recognize them....Every good tree bears good fruit.* Matthew 7:16,17

Or, as the verse immediately after today's passage in Ephesians puts it:

> *We are God's workmanship, created in Christ*
> *Jesus to do good works, which God prepared in*
> *advance for us to do.* Ephesians 2:10

All this to say...

You and I are not saved by works. We are saved for works.

Day 5
Active Grace

> *Love your enemies and pray for those who*
> *persecute you.* Matthew 5:44

The following is a true story. It has burned inside my heart for years and I hope someday to co-write it with the participants—two people I now count as good friends.

Judy was thoroughly committed to her son. He was her firstborn and she loved him deeply. Needless to say she was devastated when she learned of his brutal murder in a drug deal that went bad. At first she wanted to kill the murderer. Better yet, she wanted to kill his family so he'd suffer like she was suffering. She's a feisty, strong-willed woman and probably would have done it—if it wasn't for her love and commitment to Jesus Christ.

Immediately after the murder the Lord began to work with Judy, insisting that she forgive the killer. At first she refused. Gradually she gave in—but with one condition: She could not forgive him on her own. If the Lord wanted her to forgive then He must help her see the killer through His eyes, through His eyes of love.

It was a clever move on Judy's part. Basically she had

put the ball back into the Lord's court. It was out of her hands. She didn't have to deal with it. The episode was finished. Or so she thought...

Five months later she was visiting a friend in prison when she heard the clear and unmistakable voice of the Lord: "Judy," He said, "the young man who killed your son is in this room."

At first Judy thought she was crazy. She looked around but no one else heard the voice—not even the guards who were stationed on either side of her.

The Voice repeated Himself, "Judy, the young man who killed your son is in this room—and I want you to love him for Me."

Suddenly, unexplained tears were rolling down her cheeks. "Lord," she protested, "I can forgive him, but I can't love."

"Judy," the Voice interrupted, "do you love Me?"

"Lord, you know I love You. But..."

"Then love Richard for Me."

"But..."

"Judy, do you love Me?"

"Lord," she sobbed, barely able to get the words out, "You know I love You. But..."

"Then love Richard for Me."

Three times the Lord asked if she loved Him. And each time that she professed her love, He insisted that she love her son's killer.

Finally, she was broken. Uncontrollable tears of love and repentance continued to wash over her face. She slowly rose to her feet and began to walk around the room. Although she had been at the trial she could not remember the killer's face. Finally she heard, "Stop. He's right here."

She looked down and there was Richard seated beside her, a hardened killer of not one, but two human beings. But she didn't see that. By the grace of God she saw a young man (not unlike her own son) who was bound and shackled by hate and fear. And once again the tears began to pour. But this time they were not tears of repentance. They were tears of love. The Lord was indeed allowing her to see the murderer of her son through His eyes.

She knelt beside the man, introduced herself and began to share the supernatural love she felt washing over her. She told of her love and forgiveness and she told of the Lord's love. She also explained how Jesus wanted to forgive him.

Finally she was able to look up through her tears long enough to see something that took her breath away. This hardened criminal was also beginning to weep, sobbing uncontrollably.

Judy had obeyed. As a result, God's grace was flowing. But that was only the beginning...

Day 6
Pursuing Grace

I have loved you with an everlasting love; I have drawn you with loving-kindness. Jeremiah 31:3

Seeing Judy kneel beside Richard and the tears both of them were shedding, the guards quickly swooped in to drag her away. In the warden's office she was threatened. Such a breach of security (the victim's mother and the killer in the same room) must never be mentioned. She must forget ever meeting Richard. She must put the incident completely out of her mind.

But Judy couldn't. She had felt the Lord's great love for the boy, she had seen him through God's eyes. And now she had no choice. Now she couldn't stop herself. Now she loved him fiercely.

She began to write letters to Richard, sharing Scriptures, explaining the great love Jesus had for him.

But Richard did all he could to shut her up. He was the

godfather of the prison, the controller, famed for his ruthlessness. He did not need Christ. He began sending letters back to her—mean, discouraging letters—anything to get rid of her. But she would not give up. He began to get involved in drugs, the occult—anything he could do to silence her voice, and the voice of God.

But Judy wouldn't stop. More correctly the love Christ had placed in her heart wouldn't stop.

But Richard wasn't her only obstacle. There was also her family. As she continued to share Christ's love with Richard her family began to turn on her, calling her a traitor and worse. How dare she reach out to the killer of their brother! How dare she claim to love him!

Then there was her pastor who quietly tried to explain that she was "getting a little carried away with this forgiveness stuff."

And finally there were the penal authorities who made it clear that her efforts to see Richard again would never succeed. (They figured she was either crazy or wanted to kill him—or both.)

The odds were impossible. But God's pursuing grace buried deep within Judy's heart would not give up. For months and months Judy's letters kept coming to Richard. Until finally, to make a long story short, when Richard was in solitary confinement, he dropped to his knees and finally received Christ's forgiveness.

Needless to say there was lots of rejoicing between the two. But the journey wasn't over. Judy still had to deal with the officials, her family and her church. Meanwhile Richard had to disengage himself from all the power plays in prison including hostilities where his life and the lives of others were threatened.

But Judy and Richard finally did meet. And today in many ways Richard has become the son Judy had lost, while Judy has become Richard's spiritual mother, visiting him frequently at the prison.

Recently, because of illness and financial hardship, Judy has had to stop taking that 100-mile bus ride to the prison as often as she would like. But when she does get to go, and when she and Richard walk about talking to fellow inmates about the forgiving love of Jesus Christ, the inmates listen. The evidence is the many cards Judy receives every Mother's Day from her new sons in Christ Jesus.

Judy demonstrates the depth and power of Christ's grace. It is the grace that loves and saves a world. A grace we don't have to generate on our own. A grace that we only need to let flow into our hearts—and out to others.

11
THE TRUTH STANDS

But you, Bethlehem Ephrathah, though you are small among the clans of Judah, out of you will come for me one who will be ruler over Israel, whose origins are from of old, from ancient times. Micah 5:2

I recently asked one of the best writers I know why he became a Christian. His answer was simple (although perhaps a bit egotistical). "The Bible," he said, "is the only piece of writing I'd ever read that I cannot improve upon." As far as this man is concerned the Bible is artistic perfection.

But there's more perfection to the Bible than its art. It is inerrant. It is without error. It is without error historically, archaeologically and prophetically.

Let's take a fleeting glance at prophecy. As I mentioned before, there were over 300 Old Testament prophecies fulfilled in the life of Christ alone. The odds of one man fulfilling even a few dozen of these prophecies would be phenomenal, but to fulfill all 300 would be impossible! But, as usual, God has done the impossible. I won't be able to squeeze all 300 prophecies into these few paragraphs but here are just a few. As you read them, keep in mind that the passages were written hundreds of years before Christ was born.

His Birth

> *Therefore the Lord himself will give you a sign:*
> *The virgin will be with child and will give birth*
> *to a son, and will call him Immanuel* [Which
> means "God with us."] Isaiah 7:14

His Ministry While on Earth

> *He shall make it glorious, by the way of the sea,*
> *on the other side of Jordan, Galilee of the Gentiles.*
> *The people who walk in darkness*
> *Will see a great light;*
> *Those who live in a dark land,*
> *The light will shine on them.*
> Isaiah 9:1,2 (*NASB*)

> *Then will the eyes of the blind be opened and*
> *the ears of the deaf unstopped. Then will the*
> *lame leap like a deer, and the mute tongue*
> *shout for joy.* Isaiah 35:5,6

His Triumphal Entry into Jerusalem

> *Rejoice greatly, O Daughter of Zion! Shout,*
> *daughter of Jerusalem! See, your king comes to*
> *you, righteous and having salvation, gentle and*
> *riding on a donkey, on a colt, the foal of a*
> *donkey.* Zechariah 9:9

His Crucifixion

> *But he was pierced for our transgressions, he was crushed for our iniquities; the punishment that brought us peace was upon him, and by his wounds we are healed. We all, like sheep, have gone astray, each of us has turned to his own way; and the Lord has laid on him the iniquity of us all.* Isaiah 53:5,6

> *A band of evil men has encircled me, they have pierced my hands and my feet. I can count all my bones; people stare and gloat over me. They divide my garments among them and cast lots for my clothing.* Psalm 22:16-18

The existence of such prophecies and their fulfillment would be impossible unless the prophetic Scriptures themselves were 100 percent accurate.

But fulfilled prophecy is only one proof of Scripture's infallibility.

Day 2
Jesus' Perspective

> *All Scripture is inspired by God.*
> 2 Timothy 3:16 (*NASB*)

Before we get into defending the inerrancy of Scripture, let's briefly review exactly what the Scriptures say about Scripture.

For starters, they say that "all Scripture" every word in the Bible, is inspired by God. And by "inspired" we're not talking about someone getting so excited and worked up about the

Lord that they invented a bunch of tall tales to give Him glory. A more exact translation is "All Scripture is God-breathed." Somehow, someway, every word of Scripture contains the breath of God—a portion of His actual living, breathing life.

This "living" aspect of the Word leads to another quality we've already touched upon:

> *The word of God is living and active. Sharper than any double-edged sword, it penetrates even to dividing soul and spirit, joints and marrow; it judges the thoughts and attitudes of the heart.* Hebrews 4:12

Because of this living aspect, the Scriptures are used by God to save us (see Jas. 1:21), cleanse us (see Eph. 5:26), encourage us (see Rom. 15:4), give us faith (see Rom. 10:17), equip us to do good (see 2 Tim. 3:17) and help us see ourselves as we really are (see Jas. 1:23-25).

These are the claims the Bible makes about Scripture. But any book can make exaggerated claims about itself. What we need is proof. But not only proof, we also need endorsements by people we can trust.

Time doesn't permit us to go down the complete list of great scientists, humanitarians, philosophers and statesmen who have embraced and endorsed the Bible. So let's just pick the most trustworthy person...

Jesus Christ Believed

As we've seen before, Jesus was well aware of the power of Scripture—particularly when He chose to use it as His only weapon to fight Satan out there in the wilderness. In fact, despite all of what was available to them, both Jesus and Satan chose to use only God's holy Word in the great showdown (although Satan perverted God's Word and used it out of context).

But this was not the only time Christ used the Word. He often made reference to it. He used it again and again to teach, to correct, to clarify. And, most importantly, He used it as the ultimate proof of who He is and why He came.

Never once did Christ cast doubt on the Scriptures regarding their trustworthiness. In fact, He did just the opposite—He always treated the Word as it is—perfect and God-spoken.

And perhaps this is the best of all inerrant arguments. If Jesus Christ, Himself, looked upon the Scriptures as perfect and without error, then I'd say that's a good reason for you and I to do the same.

Day 3
Historical Truth

The grass withers and the flowers fall, but the word of our God stands forever. Isaiah 40:8

Countless books have been written about the historical accuracy of Scripture. In fact, it does the subject an injustice to touch upon it in this little space. But here's a little food for thought...

Oldest and Most Accurate History

Nearly all scholars will agree that the Bible is the oldest historical document in existence. And they will also agree that it is by far the most accurate record that has ever been kept. By comparing our current copies of Scripture with those that have been buried for thousands of years, they've discovered that there's virtually no difference between the ancient and the "modern" documents. This means that the historical records of the Bible have remained exact and unaltered since they were first written. Even the tricky and detailed spelling of all those Old Testament rulers has remained virtually unchanged.

Quality Reporting

The best journalists know an accurate news story is a story confirmed by two or three sources. But the confirmation in the Bible goes further. In the Gospels there are four confirmations of Christ's ministry: Matthew, Mark, Luke and John. These four men from four distinct backgrounds, wrote the Gospels at four distinct times, and from four distinct locations. Not only did all four men agree and come to the same conclusions (a miracle in itself) but their accounts of the principal actions are practically identical!

Additional Sources

But the Bible wasn't the only historical record kept. Oral traditions such as "A great flood that swept over the world" are common in the history of many cultures.

Then there are other written records—such as this one recorded by Josephus, a Jewish historian (most likely a Pharisee) who lived during or shortly after the time of Christ:

> Now there was about this time Jesus, a wise man, if it be lawful to call him a man, for he was a doer of wonderful works, a teacher of such men as receive the truth with pleasure. He drew over to him both many of the Jews, and many of the Gentiles. He was the Christ, and when Pilate, at the suggestion of the principal men among us, had condemned him to the cross, those that loved him at the first did not forsake him; for he appeared to them alive again on the third day; as the divine prophets had foretold these and ten thousand other wonderful things concerning him. And the tribe of Christians so named from him are not extinct at this day.[1]

All this to say...

When it comes to judging the Bible on a historical basis, we have nearly an airtight case in favor of its accuracy.

Day 4
Archaeological Truth

Your word, O Lord, is eternal. Psalm 119:89

When archaeology was in its infancy some tried to use it as a tool to disprove Scripture. But as this science grew and was refined, others started to realize that archaeological findings actually confirmed Scripture. And by confirming Scripture, I'm not just talking about the discovery of cities or civilizations where the Bible said they'd be, though that in itself is tremendous evidence of the accuracy of the Bible. Interestingly, archaeology goes many steps further. It even offers possible proof of miracles.

One of my favorite bits of archaeological trivia concerns Jericho—the city Joshua marched around and whose walls fell when the people shouted and blew trumpets. Now, usually, the walls of cities that were under siege always fell in, towards the city. But in the ruins of Jericho they've found that for some strange reason the walls had actually fallen outwards, away from the city. To this day no one has a suitable explanation. It's almost as if the walls had fallen by themselves. Hmmm... Now you can't go to court with this type of evidence but it does make interesting food for thought.

What does hold up in court is that there are thousands of archaeological findings that support the Bible's accuracy. Or as Nelson Glueck, whom Josh McDowell considers to be one of the three greatest archaeologists, is quoted as saying: "It may be stated categorically that no archaeological discovery has ever controverted [opposed] a biblical reference." [2]

In fact, not only is the credibility of the Bible strengthened through archaeology, but so is the faith of some of the archaeologists. Millar Burrows, a Yale archaeologist, put it best:

> Archaeological work has unquestionably strengthened confidence in the reliability of the Scriptural record. More than one archaeologist has found his respect for the Bible increased by the experience of excavation in Palestine.[3]

Day 5
The Care to Preserve Scripture

I warn everyone who hears the words of the prophecy of this book: If anyone adds anything to them, God will add to him the plagues described in this book. And if anyone takes words away from this book of prophecy, God will take away from him his share in the tree of life and in the holy city, which are described in this book. Revelation 22:18,19

Since the Bible is so old it only stands to reason that some will question it's accuracy. They think, *Surely over the centuries of copying and recopying, changes and errors have slipped in.*

You might think so. But God, in His wisdom, had other plans...

The ancient Jews actually created a special group of men whose duty was to preserve the accuracy of the writings to the finest detail. They believed they were handling God's holy Word and they took every conceivable precaution to make sure that every word, every symbol, even every letter was exactly the same as in the original manuscripts.

Here are just a few of their painstaking rules and regulations:

- The ink was prepared with a special recipe.
- The persons copying the writings had to bathe.
- They had to sit in full Jewish dress.
- Each line had to contain exactly 30 letters.
- Each consonant had to be separated by the width of a hair.
- Not a single word or letter could be written from memory.
- If they were writing the name of God and even the king came in and addressed them, they had to ignore the person speaking.
- And, if these rules (and plenty more) were not followed, the copy had to be destroyed.[4]

With such precautions it's safe to say that no creative "doctoring" was allowed to creep in.

In short, there has been no historical document in the world whose accuracy has been so carefully preserved as the Bible.

Day 6
The Dead Sea Scrolls

> "My Spirit, who is on you, and my words that I
> have put in your mouth will not depart from
> your mouth, or from the mouths of your
> children, or from the mouths of their
> descendants from this time on and forever,"
> says the Lord. Isaiah 59:21

The discovery of the Dead Sea Scrolls gives us another reason to believe that the Bible we have today is the same as the one God originally inspired. In 1947 a shepherd boy stumbled on a cave with several hidden jars that contained scrolls of Scriptures (including the entire book of Isaiah). When scientists investigated those scrolls, they found some to date as far back as 120 B.C.!

At last it was time for the great showdown. If our Bible was the same as those Scriptures that were over 2,000 years old, it would prove that God's Word had remained unchanged from the time God first inspired it. But if those Scriptures were different from our Bible, it would prove that people had tampered with God's Word over the centuries and that it could no longer be trusted. Carefully the experts went over the text—back and forth, checking every phrase, every word, every letter. They knew the gravity of their findings.

And the result?

According to Gleason Archer in his *Survey of the Old Testament*, the Isaiah scrolls proved to be identical to the modern Hebrew Bible in more than 95 percent of the text. The five percent variation consisted of obvious slips of the pen and variations of spelling.

The test had been passed. In over 2,000 years the Word of God had remained virtually unchanged![5]

Not only is Scripture the actual God-breathed Word of our Lord, but many many scholars agree that it is the most accurate and perfect book ever written.

Even the harshest critic (if he or she is educated) will admit that there is absolutely no historical book of such honesty and integrity. But as weighty as their opinions may be they mean nothing in comparison to what Jesus Christ believed—or to what the Scriptures themselves teach when they say, "All Scripture is God-breathed" (2 Tim. 3:16).

Footnotes

1. McDowell, Josh, as quoted in *Evidence That Demands a Verdict*, (San Bernardino: Here's Life Publishers, 1972) p. 82.
2. *Evidence*, p. 65.
3. *Evidence*, p. 66.
4. According to *Hebrew Text of the Old Testament* by Samuel Davidson, as quoted in *Evidence that Demands a Verdict*, pp. 56,57.
5. Myers, Bill, *Hot Topics, Tough Questions*, (Wheaton: SP Publications, Inc., 1987) p. 77.

12
THE MANY FACES OF COMPASSION

Day 1
The Man of Sorrows

Surely he took up our infirmities and carried our sorrows. Isaiah 53:4

There's another aspect of Christ's love and sacrifice we haven't really looked into yet. It has to do with carrying our sorrows. Not only did Jesus suffer for and carry the sorrow of our sins when He was on the cross, but for 33 years He also carried and endured the full load of humanness here on earth. For 33 years He endured all of its pain, all of its sorrow and all of its temptations.

This is what's so vitally important for us to remember: God is not some circus ringmaster with a snapping whip who demands we jump through His rings of righteousness. He's been here. He knows the hell we've created for ourselves here on earth. From firsthand experience He understands all of our struggles. This is what the writer of Hebrews meant when he wrote:

> *For we do not have a high priest who is unable to sympathize with our weaknesses, but we have one who has been tempted in every way,*

> *just as we are—yet was without sin. Let us then*
> *approach the throne of grace with confidence, so*
> *that we may receive mercy and find grace to*
> *help us in our time of need.* Hebrews 4:15,16

Jesus Christ has borne our sorrows—on the cross, yes, but also in our day-to-day troubles. He has been tempted and has struggled in every area we will ever face. He knows what we are going through. And from personal experience He knows how to help us win.

Even when we fail and lose, He is not a demanding God with arms crossed and a foot tapping impatiently at our shortcomings. Jesus is not a Gestapo. He is a caring and feeling Coach. Someone who partners alongside us, urging us to try, strengthening to succeed and tenderly picking us up and holding us if we fail.

We are not in this alone. We have Someone fully acquainted with our sorrows. And Someone whose love and compassion is so intense that He'll come alongside us and help us bear those sorrows every minute of every day.

Day 2
Passionate Compassion

> *But now, this is what the Lord says—he who*
> *created you, O Jacob, he who formed you, O*
> *Israel: "Fear not, for I have redeemed you; I*
> *have summoned you by name; you are*
> *mine....Everyone who is called by my name,*
> *whom I created for my glory, whom I formed*
> *and made."* Isaiah 43:1,7

The greatest works of art are those that have been created with the greatest passion. When an artist truly pours himself into his work, rejoicing over its strength, agonizing over its weakness, infusing his very personality into the work, that work will capture a piece of his soul. That is the art that lasts—the masterpiece that has a part of the artist's life living and breathing on the canvas, in the marble, on the written page.

I believe this is the type of compassion the Lord has for us. He has poured His very life into us and is absolutely passionate when it comes to defending and protecting us. I believe this is why He hates sin so intensely and this is why He is so angry when He sees us destroying ourselves and others with that sin.

When I was a boy my family moved from the city into the country. It seemed all my new friends thought it was their mission in life to try to educate and impress the city slicker. One fellow in particular did just that. But not necessarily the way he had planned.

He was showing me around his dairy farm. No doubt he saw my citified eyes widen as we approached the bull pen. So, to impress me, the kid climbed on the bull's fence and began shouting and teasing. But that wasn't good enough. Soon he climbed to the top and straddled the fence as he carried on his taunt with death. Luckily it was short-lived.

Out of nowhere the hired hand appeared. He reached over, grabbed my friend, pulled him off the fence and dragged him to the ground. Then, with a quick kick to the pants and swearing a blue streak, he made it painfully clear that he never wanted to catch my friend on that fence again.

Why such harsh treatment? Because he loved that kid. He loved him and was passionately committed to his welfare. He was outraged; he was absolutely livid to see the boy treat so cheaply the life the man loved so dearly.

I think of that incident from time to time and can't help but wonder if that is the type of passion my Father has for my well-being. Because He loves me He will do whatever is necessary to make sure I don't destroy myself with sin.

Now granted, to compare God with an outraged

farmhand may not be all that accurate. But in some ways I wonder if their love and compassion are all that dissimilar.

And, interestingly enough, the farmhand, like the Lord, had definitely made his point. In fact, to the best of my knowledge, my friend never so much as touched that bull pen again.

Day 3
Compassionate Outrage

> *In the temple courts he found men selling cattle, sheep and doves, and others sitting at tables exchanging money. So he made a whip out of cords, and drove all from the temple area, both sheep and cattle; he scattered the coins of the money changers and overturned their tables. To those who sold doves he said, "Get these out of here! How dare you turn my Father's house into a market!"* John 2:14-16

This is not the meek and mild Jesus that's so often painted for us. No soft-spoken, dewy-eyed doormat here. Jesus is furious. He was passionately outraged at what had been done in His Father's house.

But why? If God is a God of love, how could He turn so angry—throwing the coins to the floor, flipping over tables, even driving merchants out with a whip? I mean come on, this doesn't sound like love to me.

But it was.

Hundreds, perhaps thousands of people a day were being ripped off by the Temple merchants. These people were sincere, dedicated, pilgrims who had traveled hundreds of miles to worship God. But instead of pasturing this dedicated flock, the leaders were fleecing it!

For one thing, the sacrificial animals the people brought

with them were seldom judged "perfect enough" to sacrifice by the Temple officials. (The fact that these officials had a side business selling "unblemished" replacement sacrifices might have clouded their judgment slightly.)

Then there was the problem of the people's "dirty money." Before they could do business in God's holy Temple and buy the official's animals for sacrifice, that awful, worldly money had to be exchanged for "clean money."

In short, if he played his cards right, a greedy Temple official could turn an 1800 percent profit per customer!

No wonder Christ was outraged! People who came to His Father out of love were being stolen blind. And I believe His feelings then are no different from His feelings today. I believe Christ feels that same burning passion inside His heart every time He sees His beloved hurt, abused or fleeced. And that is love.

Christ's compassion comes in many forms. For those who are dedicated to Him, it appears as soft encouragements and embraces. For those who are abusing and destroying those He loves, it comes as a whip.

Day 4
The Look of Compassion

He had no beauty or majesty to attract us to him, nothing in his appearance that we should desire him. He was despised and rejected by men, a man of sorrows and familiar with suffering. Like one from whom men hide their faces he was despised, and we esteemed him not. Isaiah 53:2,3

It has always fascinated me that with all that is written about Jesus in the Bible, there are only two descriptions of what He looked like here on earth. Only two. And both describe Him at the height of His compassion, when, in His intense love for us, He was pouring out His life.

The first description is in today's reading of Isaiah. The other is found in the Psalms:

> *I am poured out like water, and all my bones*
> *are out of joint. My heart has turned to wax; it*
> *has melted away within me. My strength is*
> *dried up like a potsherd, and my tongue sticks to*
> *the roof of my mouth....They have pierced my*
> *hands and my feet. I can count all my bones.*
> Psalm 22:14-17

That's it. Those are the only two physical descriptions we have of Jesus Christ while He was here on earth. Nothing about His height, His weight, His hair or facial features. Nothing.

It's as if the Holy Spirit in His great wisdom as a writer, wanted us only to focus on one thing. It's as if He only wanted us to picture our Lord and Savior when He was at the height of His compassion.

All we see are a suffering face, a body whose blood is being poured out like water, whose bones are pulled out of joint and whose hands and feet are pierced. This is the only picture painted for us. No handsome face, no piercing eyes, no towering strength—simply a man in the agonizing throes of death. A man in the midst of total and consuming compassion for us.

Day 5
The Sacrifice of Compassion

> *My command is this: Love each other as I have*
> *loved you. Greater love has no one than this, that*
> *he lay down his life for his friends.* John 15:12,13

We toss the word "love" around like it's some kind of Frisbee. Unfortunately, because of that, it carries about as much weight.

Yet the clear and distinct command from Christ is to love. It's important to keep in mind that He wasn't making some sort of suggestion or stating a great ideal. It is a boldfaced, in capital letters, front page command: LOVE.

But how much? I mean there are various degrees of love, right?

Right, and Jesus gives us the exact degree when He said, "Love each other as I have loved you."

But that concept means little to me. How can I love someone like Jesus loves me? How many opportunities am I going to have to be crucified to save a friend's life?

None. But there are other sacrifices we can make, sacrifices the Lord expects us to make.

What about giving up that business deal and actually allowing your brother in Christ to get the upper hand?

You might think, *But he's nothing but ambition. I mean all he cares about is himself!*

And exactly who did the disciples care for when they deserted Jesus after His arrest? Yet He still died for them.

What about sacrificing a grade, or missing a paper deadline to help that sister study for tomorrow's exam?

You might think, *But she's been too busy playing. She deserves a bad grade!*

Right, and we were busy sinning although Jesus died for us. We deserve death.

Or what about the sacrifice of a phone call or a humble letter of reconciliation to one of our enemies?

No way! If you would have seen what he did to me—if you would have known how he hurt me—you wouldn't even be asking. Besides I was entirely right.

Probably. But if there's anybody who was "entirely right" it was Jesus. Yet He still loved His disciples, even as they betrayed Him, denied Him and deserted Him. It seemed everyone was doing all they could to destroy and deny Christ. But He still died for them.

These days there aren't many crosses to leap upon. But there are the continual day-to-day sacrifices that Jesus expects us to make for our brothers and sisters.

Love isn't always a cozy gooey feeling. I'm sure Jesus wasn't feeling warm fuzzies when He allowed Himself to be tortured to death for us. Sometimes love is just plain, old-fashioned, excruciatingly difficult, obedience. But that is what He calls for:

> *My command is this: Love each other as I have loved you.* John 15:12

Day 6
Compassion for Self?

Love your neighbor as yourself. Matthew 19:19

For years I've heard that this verse is proof that we should love ourselves. For years I've heard that our number one problem in life is that we don't love ourselves enough. For years I've heard that if we just relaxed and loved ourselves, all of our emotional hang ups would be over.

And for years I almost fell for that line. But not quite. I just couldn't equate it with what Scripture had to say about loving self:

> *But mark this: There will be terrible times in the last days. People will be lovers of themselves, lovers of money, boastful, proud, abusive, disobedient to their parents, ungrateful, unholy.* 2 Timothy 3:1,2

And the list goes on. But notice what is at the top of the

list: "lovers of themselves." Here's another catchy little verse, a direct quote from Jesus:

The man who loves his life will lose it, while the man who hates his life in this world will keep it for eternal life. John 12:25

Does this mean I'm supposed to go around with my head hanging down, always hating myself and never loving me?

Yes and no. You see as Christians we are kind of schizophrenic. There is a part of us that is regenerated, reborn and full of the Spirit of Christ. But there is also a part of us that is putrid, self-centered and dying flesh that hasn't yet given up to Jesus.

This second part is the part I hate. This second part is the part that makes me angry and that I loathe so intensely (not enough to give it over to Jesus and let it die yet, but I'm getting there). This is the "old man." The one that's constantly fighting, trying to hold me back. He'll do anything to try to stay alive—even disguise himself at being religious. But every day as I abide in Christ, that old man dies a little more and the "new man" takes a little more ground.

It is this new man that I love. He's the one I rejoice over when he does right—when he loves, when he worships, when he obeys, when he gives part of his life to others.

Even at that it's not really me I'm loving. It's the Jesus part in me. Still, I'm not going to get a headache trying to divide the difference. No matter how you word it, the point is, as Christ takes over more and more of my life, I am filled with more and more of His peace, His joy and most importantly, His love.

And loving Jesus is a thousand times better than loving myself.

13
A VICTORIOUS FUTURE

The Lord will be king over the whole earth. On that day there will be one Lord, and his name the only name. Zechariah 14:9

Picture it.

One day Jesus Christ will return—not as a suffering savior on a cross, but as a ruling King on the throne. The world Satan has ruled and oppressed will be turned back to its original Owner. And the original Owner will realign and adjust everything He created to function as it was originally designed.

No longer will there be twisted contortions of what were once beautiful creations. No longer will love be contorted into lust, holiness twisted into self-righteousness or a relationship with God distorted into religion.

And our contributions to His Creation? The sickness, disease and death that we've managed to introduce through our own sin? They will be totally eliminated.

In short the "groaning creation" will finally be set free. It will once again function as it was designed to function and be the blessing it was intended to be.

Once we were like a magnificent and precisely tuned

orchestra. There was no end to the beauty and wonder our music could create under the expert hands of our Conductor.

But, being persuaded to believe our Conductor was a tyrant, we threw Him off the podium. Now we had freedom. Now we could play whatever we wanted to play, whenever we wanted to play it.

But our music became discordant, off tempo and out of tune. We had no leader. No one could agree on anything. We broke into factions. Each group trying to overpower the other. In our refusal to work together we even forgot the range and unique abilities of each of our instruments. Drums were trying to play flute lines. Violins were trying to be tubas. Soon screeching, squawks and unbearable thunderings replaced what was once breathtaking beauty. And soon the very orchestra that was created to bring beauty and joy brought nothing but ugliness and pain.

But not forever. Eventually many in the orchestra realized what we had done and asked the Conductor to again lead. And for many of us, He has done just that—at least in part.

But soon He will return and take complete charge. When He does we will be able to play the full range of our instruments in perfect harmony with all of our fellow orchestra members. We will be part of the beauty and majesty He originally created us to be.

Day 2
Another Description

Among the lampstands was someone "like a son of man," dressed in a robe reaching down to his feet and with a golden sash around his chest. His head and hair were white like wool, as white as snow, and his eyes were like blazing fire. His feet were like bronze glowing in a furnace, and his voice was like the sound of

*rushing waters. In his right hand he held seven
stars, and out of his mouth came a sharp
double-edged sword. His face was like the sun
shining in all its brilliance.* Revelation 1:13-16

I mentioned before that there are only a couple descriptions of what Jesus looked like on earth. But there are other descriptions. Descriptions of what He looks like in heaven and later on when He returns to earth. Now that He is in heaven, He is no longer the tormented, suffering Savior. And when He returns we will see Him as He really is—a powerful and conquering King. Today's reading conveys some of that awesome and terrifying power. In fact, John ends this passage with his reaction to what he saw:

*When I saw him, I fell at his feet as though
dead.* Revelation 1:17

Just as the Holy Spirit wants us to understand that the first Jesus seen on earth was full of mercy and compassion, it seems He's making it equally clear that the next Jesus will be full of awesome power, glory and majesty.

We no longer have a suffering, broken and bleeding Christ for our King. Today Christ sits on His throne full of awesome power and unutterable glory!

Day 3
The Conquering Warrior

*I saw heaven standing open and there before me
was a white horse, whose rider is called Faithful
and True. With justice he judges and makes
war. His eyes are like blazing fire, and on his
head are many crowns. He has a name written
on him that no one knows but he himself. He is*

> *dressed in a robe dipped in blood, and his name
> is the Word of God. The armies of heaven were
> following him, riding on white horses and
> dressed in fine linen, white and clean. Out of
> his mouth comes a sharp sword with which to
> strike down the nations. "He will rule them
> with an iron scepter." He treads the winepress of
> the fury of the wrath of God Almighty. On his
> robe and on his thigh he has this name written:*
>
> *KING OF KINGS AND LORD OF LORDS.*
>
> Revelation 19:11-16

The first time Jesus arrived in Jerusalem He came riding on a donkey, the symbol of a peaceful king.

The next time He makes His entrance things will be a little different. The next time He will be coming as a conquering warrior!

I saw a bumper sticker a while back that made me smile and shudder at the same time. It simply read:

> Jesus is coming back—and boy, is He mad.

I don't know about others, but I'd much rather bow my knee and submit to Him now than when He returns blazing with the wrath and fury of God Almighty!

Day 4
A People-Pleasing Cure

> *Do not be afraid of those who kill the body but
> cannot kill the soul. Rather, be afraid of the One
> who can destroy both soul and body in hell.*
> Matthew 10:28

I am a first class, triple A, people pleaser. I wish I wasn't but I am. I mean my idea of heaven would be for everyone to come up and slap me on the back (not all at once, mind you) and tell me what a great, super-neat guy I am.

But the problem is—I live in fear. Fear of what people think. I particularly live in fear of the rich and powerful because they're the ones who seem to have the most control over my life.

But I've found a cure.

As I keep growing in Christ, I've found the best freedom from my bondage comes when I look squarely at my Lord. That freedom comes when I begin to dwell on exactly who He is. And as I begin to see His power, His glory, His awesome holiness, suddenly the hold other people have on my life begins to weaken. And by comparing how their power will stand up to Jesus Christ's power, well, I quickly realize there's no contest about who I really want to please.

> *Then the kings of the earth, the princes, the
> generals, the rich, the mighty, and every slave and
> every free man hid in caves and among the rocks
> of the mountains. They called to the mountains
> and the rocks, "Fall on us and hide us from the
> face of him who sits on the throne and from the
> wrath of the Lamb! For the great day of their
> wrath has come, and who can stand?"*
> Revelation 6:15-17

Day 5
You Can't Keep a Good God Down

> *Then he got into the boat and his disciples
> followed him. Without warning, a furious
> storm came up on the lake, so that the waves
> swept over the boat. But Jesus was sleeping. The*

> *disciples went and woke him, saying, "Lord,*
> *save us! We're going to drown!"*
> *He replied, "You of little faith, why are you so*
> *afraid?" Then he got up and rebuked the winds*
> *and the waves, and it was completely calm.*
> *The men were amazed and asked, "What kind*
> *of man is this? Even the winds and the waves*
> *obey him!"* Matthew 8:23-27

Even when Jesus was in human form here on earth there were still times His divinity couldn't help but shine through.

Over the next two days as we close our studies together, let's take a look at some of those times—not so we can be awed by the miracles or special effects, but so we can be reminded that today, at this very moment, Christ is the Conquering King. Today, Jesus Christ can invade our hopeless, natural situations with His supernatural power and strength. We don't have to wait until He returns to solve our problems. He operated mightily when He was first here on earth, and He still operates mightily today.

Power for Provision

> *He told the crowd to sit down on the ground.*
> *Then he took the seven loaves and the fish, and*
> *when he had given thanks, he broke them and*
> *gave them to the disciples, and they in turn to*
> *the people. They all ate and were satisfied.*
> *Afterward the disciples picked up seven*
> *basketfuls of broken pieces that were left over.*
> *The number of those who ate was four*
> *thousand, besides women and children.*
> Matthew 15:35-38

Like most of my baby boomer buddies I'm running in front of a giant rolling boulder—bigger and faster than

Indiana Jones ever had to worry about. In fact I'm sure it's going to crush me if I just stop and rest for even the briefest second. Its name? "Finances."

And yet, time and time again I read that if I seek God (as the people in today's reading were doing) and obey Him, He can take my meager little provisions and supernaturally turn them into abundance.

I can't seem to remember this all of the time. But the times I do remember are the times that I experience His peace, His joy and, most importantly, His rest.

Power over Evil

> *Even while the boy was coming, the demon*
> *threw him to the ground in a convulsion. But*
> *Jesus rebuked the evil spirit, healed the boy and*
> *gave him back to his father. And they were all*
> *amazed at the greatness of God.* Luke 9:42,43

If Jesus Christ can cast demons out, and destroy all of the strongholds of Satan, can He not destroy the evil in me?

What an encouragement it is to know that Jesus has complete power over evil. And, as I submit myself to Him, He will remove any evil in my life.

Day 6
More Kingly Power

Power over Sickness

> *Jesus went throughout Galilee, teaching in their*
> *synagogues, preaching the good news of the*
> *kingdom, and healing every disease and*
> *sickness among the people. News about him*
> *spread all over Syria, and people brought to him*

> *all who were ill with various diseases, those*
> *suffering severe pain, the demon-possessed,*
> *those having seizures, and the paralyzed, and*
> *he healed them.* Matthew 4:23,24

Not once in all of His ministry did Jesus refuse to heal someone. There were times He left regions because there was so little faith, but we do not have a single account of Jesus saying, "You're suffering? Too bad, I'm not in the mood."

Does this mean Jesus always heals today?

No.

Why not?

You got me. But I do know this. For those who are earnestly seeking Him, Jesus will do one of two things. He will either heal them or He will give them the strength and peace to eventually use their illness for good and for His glory. Those illness will in one way or another be changed from destruction to construction—either through healing or by eventually using it to minister to others and to glorify God.

Power over Death

> *As he approached the town gate, a dead person*
> *was being carried out—the only son of his*
> *mother, and she was a widow. And a large*
> *crowd from the town was with her. When the*
> *Lord saw her, his heart went out to her and he*
> *said, "Don't cry."*
> *Then he went up and touched the coffin, and*
> *those carrying it stood still. He said, "Young*
> *man, I say to you, get up!" The dead man sat*
> *up and began to talk, and Jesus gave him back*
> *to his mother.* Luke 7:12-15

There are several accounts of Jesus raising someone from the dead: this widow's son, a ruler's little girl and His own friend Lazarus. That's some track record.

Today each of us has suffered death—death of dreams, relationships or loved ones. Yet we can rest assured that Jesus has the power to resurrect—maybe not on our terms or by our timetable. But, Jesus Christ has the power to change death into life—no matter what that death may be.

Power to Forgive

> *Some men brought to him a paralytic, lying on a mat. When Jesus saw their faith, he said to the paralytic, "Take heart, son; your sins are forgiven."*
>
> *At this, some of the teachers of the law said to themselves, "This fellow is blaspheming!"*
>
> *Knowing their thoughts, Jesus said, "Why do you entertain evil thoughts in your hearts? Which is easier: to say, 'Your sins are forgiven,' or to say, 'Get up and walk'? But so that you may know that the Son of Man has authority on earth to forgive sins...." Then he said to the paralytic, "Get up, take your mat and go home." And the man got up and went home.* Matthew 9:2-7

For me there are few stories in Scripture that capture the full ministry of Jesus Christ as this one. First, He emphasized His power to forgive.

He has the power to forgive whatever we have done and whatever we may do. If we sincerely confess and repent He will forgive us of anything.

Then there was His grace. From the passage, we know of nothing the man did to earn forgiveness and healing. He simply came to the source of grace. And that was enough.

Christ's forgiveness and grace are more than just fire insurance from hell. His grace and forgiveness are active now, now in the very midst of our day-to-day lives.

It's true, as the conquering King, Jesus offers us a terrific eternity. But that's just for starters. He also offers us a terrific now—maybe not always in outward circumstances, but always, deep inside, where we really live. You and I can have a life "perfect and complete, lacking in nothing" right here on earth (Jas. 1:4, *NASB*). Not only do we have a terrific eternity in heaven in store for our future, but we can also have a terrific now. Or as Jesus, Himself, said...

> *I have come that they may have life, and have it to the full.* John 10:10.